CW01510157

MONUMENTA
ESTONICA

ESTONIAN ENCYCLOPAEDIA PUBLISHERS·TALLINN·1996

Rein Zobel

WALLS AND TOWERS OF TALLINN

ESTONIAN ENCYCLOPAEDIA PUBLISHERS·TALLINN·1996

MONUMENTA ESTONICA
Editor of the series: Professor Rein Zobel

Translator: Margareta Telliskivi de Villacís
Editor: Elo Lutsepp
Design: Aarne Mesikäpp
Photos: Viivi Ahonen, Gustav German, Ene Kull, Boris Mäemets, Viktor Salmre, Ann Tenno, Rein Zobel
English editor: Mari Ets
Art editor: Anne Järve
Layout: Rein Aro

Front cover: *Wall section bordering on the St. Michael's nunnery*
Back cover: *Kiek in de Kök. View from the Ingrian Bastion*
Title page: *Tallinn in 1688. A painting on the casket of the Tallinn Town Council's documents*

ISSN 1406 - 071X
ISBN 5 - 89900 - 039 - 2

Printed in Estonia by Tallinn Book Printers in 1996

Medieval Tallinn was both an administrative and a trade centre. The buildings that formed the heart of that centre, the present Old Town, are therefore situated in two differently planned and built parts, the hilltop fortress of Toompea and the lower town.

The fortress of Toompea, on a high limestone plateau, which was originally an Estonian earthen stronghold named *Lyndanise*, later known as the Danish *Castrum Danorum* and the German *Ordensburg*, was in its turn divided into two settlements. The main fortress, the so-called Small Castle (*castrum minus, Schloss*) was the residence of the representative of the supreme power, who was either the King's regent or the ruling order master and his henchmen. The Great Castle (*castrum majus*) or the Episcopal Castle was, first and foremost, a centre of local ecclesiastical power, but also the site of the town residences of the local feudal lords and an abode of a number of local merchants and craftsmen. Both areas were well defended and united by outworks (*cingele, Zwinger*), located in the southern part of the plateau. The outer ward was a complex structure with gateways leading both to Tõnismägi (*Tönnisberg*), a settlement on the outskirts of Toompea, and to the lower town. Land rights and chivalric privileges were valid in Toompea, this part of the town lived independently from the lower town.

The lower town (*suburbium, Unterstadt*), better known as the Hanseatic town Reval, was a relatively independent port and a trade centre throughout the Middle Ages. The lower town was populated by merchants and craftsmen, and a large number of lower class people depending on them. In 1238/48, Lübeck city rights Tallinn codex (*codex Revaliensis*) was enacted here. The life of the city was governed by the magistracy or the city council (*magistratus, Rath*). The population of Tallinn mostly consisted of Germans and Estonians, but also Swedes and Finns, and a smaller number of Russians and other nations. Latin was the official language of the city until mid-14th century, after that, until the end of the Middle Ages, it was Middle Low German (*Mittel-Niederdeutsch*). The spoken language was often a mixture of Low German and Estonian. This fact, along with many others concerning the older history of Tallinn, is proven by the unusually well preserved city archive.

By the end of the Middle Ages, in the 1530s, the area of Tallinn was 36.7 hectares, of which the fortress of Toompea was 7.4 hectares, and the lower town 29.3 hectares. Both living areas were surrounded by a strong defensive zone. During late Middle Ages, the area of the

5

fortifications, the Order Castle excluded, was 14.2 hectares, or 28 per cent of the total area of the fortified centre. The fortifications of the lower town, 11 hectares, made up most of the defensive zone. This publication discusses namely the medieval fortifications of the lower town, better known as the town wall of Tallinn (*Revaler Stadtmauer*). The history of the planning and architectural development of these fortifications is both extensive and complex. It began in the era of catapults and other projectiles and cold steel, following all the stages of development, caused by changes in urban construction, architecture and military technique, and especially the introduction of firearms in the second half of the 14th century. First steps toward the erection of successive layers of walls had been taken by the end of the Middle Ages and from the 16th to the 19th century, mighty fortification complexes were set up. Then, the importance of the medieval fortifications declined until they were rediscovered, this time as heritage.

In this book, the development of the medieval fortifications of Tallinn is outlined according to the historical succession of rulers, with information on the geographical, historical and political background.

Until 1219: PREHISTORY

Most probably Tallinn became known as a port and trade centre in the 10th century, when the range of long-distance trading increased in the Baltic Sea area. Since the sea level was 2.5—3 metres higher than it is now, the sandy beach in the region of the present Uus Street could be used as a port. The area was protected from storm winds by a 12-metre sandstone bank and by a small cape, covered by boulders, which continued as a reef in the sea towards north-east.

The earthen stronghold by the Pirita River, built in the 6th century by the Estonians from the Rävala district, was located about 10 kilometres from the new port. When the stronghold was destroyed by fire in 1030, the place was neglected and a new stronghold, named Lyndanise (meaning 'the site of a stronghold'), was erected near the new port. The eastern neighbours called the new stronghold Koluvan (*Kolōvan=Kalevanlinna=Kalevi linnus*/Kalev's stronghold). This name was probably also used by the Sicilian geographer al-Idrisi on his map of the world from 1154. Lyndanise was built on the Toompea plateau that was nearly 30 metres higher than its surroundings, but the exact location of the stronghold is unfortunately not known.

By the 13th century, a Scandinavian tradeyard and Oleviste (*St. Olaf's, St. Olai*) merchants' church (*ecclesia mercatorum*) had been set up by the port. Nearby was the Russian yard (*konets*) with the so-called old Russian church. The market place was probably at the site of the present Town Hall Square. The church or chapel of the christianised Estonians, the Holy Ghost (*St. Spiritus, Heiligengeist*), was located near the market place. The settlement was covered by a network of roads. A road led from the port to the stronghold, another main trade route branched along the Karja (Cattle) streets into main roads leading

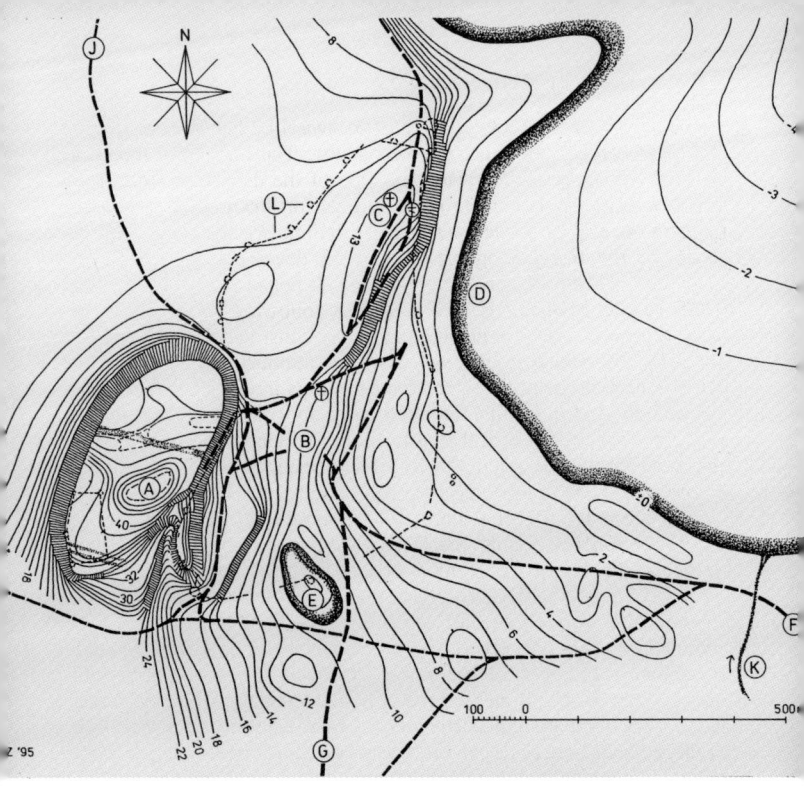

Topographical scheme of Tallinn, approx. 1200 (reconstruction)
A — the limestone plateau of Toompea, B — market place and church, C — Scandinavian and Russian tradeyards and churches, D — the site of the port, E — a marshy lake, F — road to Viru and Järva counties (Tartu road), G — road to Harju and Lääne counties (Pärnu road), H — road to north-west Estonia (Paldiski road), J — road to Kalamaja, K — the Härjapea /Oxhead River, L — the town wall and its towers at present, -4 ...40 sea depth, coast line and relief at the beginning of the 13th century

towards Pärnu (Lihula) and Tartu (Narva). The latter led both to Pskov and Novgorod. It is supposed that foreign merchants already spent their winters in Tallinn. Estonians who were mainly peasants probably spent their winters in their home villages, most of which were quite far from the sea. Although Estonia got its first bishop from Sweden already in 1165 and some Estonians had been christianised, the majority of the native population were still heathens.

1219—1226: THE FIRST DANISH ERA

In the course of the crusade (*Nordische Mission*), proclaimed in 1208 to christianise and subordinate Estonia and Livonia, Danish King Waldemar II and his allies occupied Lyndanise stronghold in June 1219. The revenge battle three days later, although cunningly planned by Es-

tonians from Rävala, was unsuccessful. The King had the old stronghold pulled down and erected the wooden Taanilinnus /Danish Castle
at Toompea. Estonians' repeated attempts to re-conquer the stronghold
in 1219, 1221 and in the spring and summer of 1223 failed. The locations of the Danish stronghold and the first church the Danes built at
Toompea are not known.

1226—1227: PONTIFICAL STATE

This is a short period of internal confrontations, during which the
Papal legate Wilhelm of Modena tried to establish a Pontifical State
between the possessions of Germans and Danes, who were quarrelling
over the northern part of Estonia. The attempt failed. It is known that at
that time Tallinn was populated by Danes, Estonians, Swedes and other nations.

1227—1238: THE FIRST ORDER ERA

The Order of the Brotherhood of the Sword (*Schwertbrüder Orden,
Fratres Militiae Christi*, 1202—1237), based in Riga and set up to
submit Livonian, Latvian and Estonian heathens, seized the Danish
stronghold at Toompea. In the following years, the Brothers of the Sword
built the first stone stronghold there. It was probably a simple oblong
castle with stone walls and a corner tower, situated in the same place
as the following castles. The castle was built of local Ordovician limestone. The quarry of the stone has been found at the site of the cathedral at Toompea. Limestone from that quarry was also used for burning
lime. This major building probably inspired the first traditions of limestone architecture in Tallinn.

The lower town probably also started to grow during the first order
era. This supposition is proven by the fact that many craftsmen owned
land near the Town Hall Square, which was then the market place. It is
also possible that the first Cistercian and Dominican cloister yards had
been set up by the time. It is not known whether this development was
based on the 'Estonian law' (*ius Estonicum*) or some other settlement
privileges. As later questions concerned with *ius Estonicum* prove, most
of the buildings in the lower town were wooden.

In 1230, a major settlement policy decision was taken. To secure
its power in the lower town, the Order invited 200 German merchants
from Visby, Gotland, to live in Tallinn. 40 of them were granted fiefs in
Järvamaa district as well. The merchants probably set up the first German tradeyard and Niguliste (St. Nicholas') church, that also functioned
as castle church (*ecclesia castellatum*). The merchants and the local craftsmen were granted plots of land around the former heart of the settlement
and market place. The area covered with buildings in the centre of the
town increased considerably, at the same time preserving the network of
old road-like streets while planning the town. As a result, a circular
system of streets (Rataskaevu — Pikk — Pühavaimu — Vene (Munga)
— Vanaturg — Niguliste) was created, which was linked to the heart

of the settlement by a number of shorter radial streets.

This settlement was probably based on privileges granted by the Lubeck Law, which became the main legal act adopted in Tallinn between 1238 and 1248. Medieval Tallinn had thus become a city (1238 *civitas Revaliensis*). The city rights were exercised by the municipality (*consules civitatis*), which was formed mostly by German merchants as they were the founders of the city (*locatores*). It is worth remembering that Gotland was one of the main links in the trade chain leading both to Pskov and to Novgorod. Visby, the capital of Gotland, was a city already a hundred years before Tallinn (Reval) grew into one, and also before the Hanseatic centre Lubeck became known. After their arrival in 1230, the new settlers from Gotland quickly turned Tallinn into a Scandinavian-type urban centre. The old Tallinn is often referred to as the daughter city of Visby.

1238—1346: THE SECOND DANISH ERA

According to the Stensby treaty between Waldemar II and the meanwhile established Livonian Order, Tallinn and the neighbouring counties of Harjumaa and Virumaa were returned to Denmark. The area was a province at first, but in 1271 it became the Duchy of Estonia, with Tallinn as the capital. Toompea and the lower town, representing two parts of a city with completely different interests, as typical of the feudal order, started to develop rapidly. Late romanesque style prevailed in architecture.

The beginning of the period is characterised by the erection of a church and cloister circle (*Kirchen- und Klösterkranz*) around the heart of the city (market place) and gradual filling the gaps between them with new buildings. In 1246, the Dominicans were granted a lot in Vene (Russian) Street (then named Monk Street — *platea monachorum*) to build St. Catherine's monastery. Cistercians were given the right to build Mihkli (St. Michaeli) nunnery at the site of the 13th century Venceslaus chapel in the north-western outskirts of the town. A lot at the corner of Pühavaimu and Vene streets belonging to Kärkna (Falkenau) Cistercians was recorded in 1265, some others in Vene Street, owned by the Cistercians from Padise (Dünamünde) and Roma (Gutvalla) in 1280. The lots were probably granted long before they were recorded, possibly soon after the conquest.

To complete the picture, there follows a list of buildings and institutions that in the 2nd half of the 14th century were considered 'old', originating from earlier periods: the old town hall (*olde rathus*), old gaol (*olde bodelje*), old workshop (*olde marstall*) and old mint (*olde munte*). In the 13th century the German merchants founded a market place on the crossroad, which was situated on an old circular road and also on a crescent leading to Niguliste church on one hand, and to the port, on the other hand. A hundred years later it was called 'lower market' (*forum inferior*) or 'old market' (*dat olde market*). Most probably this market was established in order to overshadow the existing, topographically higher ancient market place at the site of the present

Town Hall Square. The latter was much more convenient for a market place, but the new settlers did not appreciate it, as the surroundings of the square were inhabited by 'non-Germans' (*Undeutsch*). Tallinn's first town hall and the first gaol were probably built near the Old Market. We can conclude that the Danish settlement had in a very short period developed into a completely functional town with all the necessary institutions. The town itself had started to grow in concentric circles.

The population of the old heart of the settlement, the so-called aldermanic town (*Ratstadt*) was under the influence of the Niguliste church and parish, the population of the northern part of the town (north of Pühavaimu /Holy Ghost church or chapel and the Cistercian properties) was under the influence of Oleviste church and parish. By the 14th century, a guild town (*Gildenstadt*) had been formed in the region influenced by Oleviste parish. The guild town lead a relatively independent life until it was united with the aldermanic town in mid-14th century.

In the middle and the second half of the 13th century, several important changes took place in the town. In the 1250s, Tallinn (Reval) became a member of a German towns trade league, and in 1280, the Hanseatic League. Dowager Queen Margrethe Sambiria, who ruled the northern part of Estonia in 1266—1282, had a positive influence on the development of the city. Her son King Eric V gave his possessions in Estonia as a fief to Margrethe, she was also granted the title of the Lady of Estonia (*domina Estoniae, en vrouve to Estland*). Tallinn got several privileges, building activities intensified.

The fortress of Toompea was rebuilt. The former castle was divided into two, the northern part was made the residence of the viceregent. In 1265, the patrimony (*Stadtmark, patrimonium*) of Tallinn was marked, covering an area of 8,230 hectares. The term 'Town and country Tallinn' (*Stadt und Land Reval*) developed. Queen Margrethe ordered further fortifications to be built. The first order to the town council and the King's vassals who resided here to secure the city with earthworks and a wall was given in 1265. Other orders followed, the Queen also saw into the financing of the constructions. For example, any man who wounded another within the limits of the patrimonium, had to pay smart-money, part of which went for the construction of the town wall (*ad murum civitatis*). The same rule applied to contract breakers. One contract imposed a fine of 'two marks for the town wall', another regulation established a fine of 'one mark for the construction of the town wall' for those who invite more guests to a wedding than allowed. In 1280, to speed up construction in Tallinn, the Queen left all rents of four years at the disposal of the city, as well as the income from the town mint, public houses and bailiffs, which formerly had gone directly to the King. The possessions of the Cistercians from Dünamünde, Roma and Kärkna in the Munga /Monk (present Vene) Street were taxed: the Queen ordered that the abbots of the cloisters had to either contribute to the building of the walls or sell their property to those who would be willing to do so.

Historical documents show thus that several measures were taken

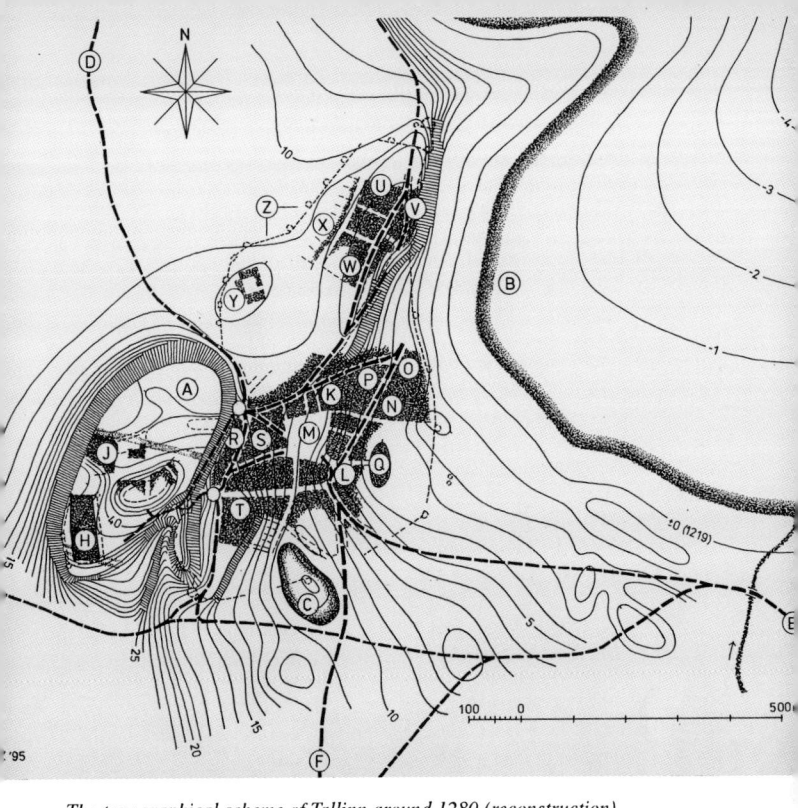

The topographical scheme of Tallinn around 1280 (reconstruction)
A — the hill of Toompea, B — the site of the port, C — a marshy lake, D — road to
Kalamaja, E — road to Viru and Järva counties, F — road to Harju and Lääne
counties, G — road to north-west Estonia, H — the Danish Castle, J — episcopal
property and St. Mary's Cathedral, K — Holy Ghost Chruch, L — the Old Mar-
ket, M —Town Hall Square, N — Dominican St.Catherine's Monastery, O — pos-
sessions of Cistercians from Padise and Roma, P — possessions of Cistercians
from Kärkna, Q — the old settlement area in Viru Street, R — the old mint, S — the
old work yard, T — Niguliste /St. Nicholas Church, U — Oleviste /St. Olaf's Church,
V — the old Russian church, W — the old company, X — possessions of vassals,
Y — the Cistercian Mihkli /St. Michael's nunnery, Z — the town wall and its
towers at present, -4 ...40 sea depth and relief

to improve the defence system of the town, probably with the aim of
building new walls in the 2nd half of the 13th century.

Research into the subject allows us to suppose that the so-called
Margrethe's wall started from the bar gate by Lühike Jalg /Short Leg,
then called Lühike Mägi (Short Hill) and continued through the lot of
Niguliste church to the Old Market and the Dominican Monastery. The
monastery yards in Vene Street were within the boundaries of the wall,
then the wall made a sharp turn to the north-west and at the site of the
Lai /Wide Street, it turned back, leading to the other bar gate by Pikk
Jalg /Long Leg, then called Pikk Mägi (Long Hill). From there, the
defensive wall continued along the scree under the slope of Toompea

11

Oleviste /St. Olaf's Church and row of defence towers on the north-western side of the town

until the Short Hill. It is necessary to add that there are no visible traces of Margrethe's wall in existence. The only known part of the defensive wall is a section of the autonomous north-western circular wall of Mihkli (St. Michael's) nunnery, which was 3.5 metres high at the turn of the 13th and 14th century.

The lower town of Tallinn reached its nearly final boundaries in the 14th century. The whole town was surrounded with a new defence system. This was a major project that could be carried out only step-by-step, according to the growth of the population and the wealth of citi-

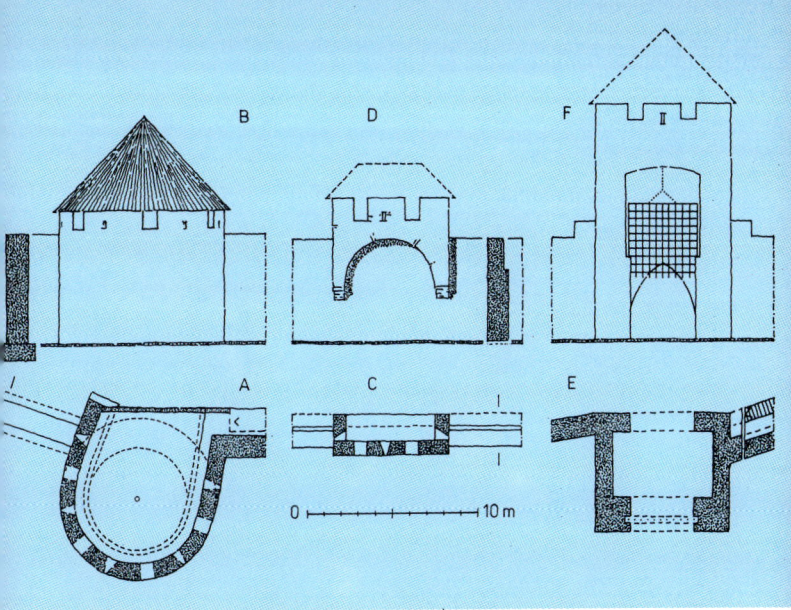

Some fortifications 1310—1320. A — defence floor of the I Kuldjala /Golden Foot Tower, B — view of the same tower, C — defence floor of the I Nunnatorn / Nun Tower, D — view of the same tower, E — ground plan of the lower part of the I Nunnavärav /Nun Gate, F — exterior of the gate tower

zens, considering historical changes and the rapid development of military technique during this century.

In a Latin document dating from 1310, legate of the Danish King Erik VI Menved, Johannes Kanne (Jens Kande), who "... by the order of the King has been given full authority to build fortifications around Tallinn", lists a number of specific orders and suggestions concerning the improvement of the defence system of the city, since " ... the city is open to conspiracy by tyrants, and is often bothered by attacks of heathens". Kanne's regulations were authorised by the King the next year. Research shows that most of these orders were carried out. Kanne had the possibility to guarantee that, because he held the position of the King's viceregent (*capitaneus*) in Toompea fortress for a long period of time.

Kanne's regulations give a high priority to connecting the so far independent possessions of the Cistercian Mihkli nunnery outside the wall with the town, as well as uniting the defence systems of the lower town with those of Toompea. Kanne allowed for the expansion of the northern part of the lower town towards the sea "... as far as wished" while in the southern part, " ... the town wall can be moved outside the moat or stay where it is or be moved back towards the centre".

Research has proven that the aldermanic town was first connected to the walls of the fortress from north and south, thus liquidating the no-man-land between the fortress and the town. Works on the northern

13

The oldest layers of the town wall can be seen between Sauna and Golden Foot towers

side were extensive: the **new wall** began 'near the old sauna' below the fortress and was connected to the circular wall of the nunnery near the site where Saunatorn /Sauna Tower was built later on. Parts of the wall, although reconstructed, have survived. The wall had a simple cross section and no loopholes, it was 6.3 metres high, 1.3 metres thick in the lower and 1 metre thick in the upper part. In the inner side of the wall, at the height of 4.3 metres, there was a step for supporting the wooden defence gallery. This is the oldest known fragment of Tallinn city wall complex, which was probably started soon after the King's resolution from 1311.

As the new town wall closed the way to Kalamaja between the fortress and the nunnery, a gate had to be built. In 1355, the gate tower was still called 'the tower near the sauna by the Long Hill' (*turris iuxta stupam sub longo monte*), but in the 1370s it was known as the Sauna Gate (*porta stoven*) or the Small Sauna Gate (*luteken bastouen porten*), about the same time, another name — **Nun Gate** (*porta monialum, süsterporte*) appeared. This name became the final name of the gate, *Süsternpforte* (Sister Gate, Nun Gate).

The gate was demolished in 1868. Existing city plans and land survey charts allow us to reconstruct the scheme of the **I stage of the Nun Gate**. The building was rectangular (7.8 by 6.7 m), had 3 floors

The supporting arch of the outer wall and the loopholes of the I Nun Tower, built in 1311—1320, can be seen in the later round tower

(height ca 13.5 m). The gate had a thoroughfare surrounded by a pointed arch-shaped portal that could be closed by a strong double door. The door was protected by an open portcullis, which could be raised and lowered from the first floor. On the top, there was an open defence floor with loopholes. From the side of the town, the tower was open. The building could probably be reached by an open staircase on its southern side.

Between the Nun Gate and the nunnery, the first known saddle tower in Tallinn, the **I Nun Tower**, was built. Since the later tower was built in a circle around the original one, the first tower can partly be seen. It was a small building, measuring 6.2 by 2.3 m at the ground level and being 8.4 m high. The only defence floor, which was open from the side of the town and could be reached by a ladder, was based on a circular racket. In three sides of the tower, there were loopholes. Its name, *Cyster-Thurm*, was first recorded in 1738. Since the nunnery had been secularised a hundred years earlier, the name must be dating from the Middle Ages. The described buildings are very similar to the town wall constructions of Visby, built a little earlier. Considering the aforementioned historical events, this seems only natural.

According to the rulings by Kanne, the sisters of the Mihkli (St. Michael's) nunnery had to build the town wall section near the convent

15

(' ... in the length of their possessions') at their own expense. Actually, they made use of their old north-western circular wall, building it just a little higher. An older building in the northern part of the wall was demolished and replaced by a two-storey *bastille*-like projecting corner tower. The tower, which can be called the **I Kuldjala /Golden Foot** (*de guldene voet*) Tower after its later name, was a horse-shoe-shaped building ($\varnothing$ 7.2 m, height ca 8 m). The only defence floor could be reached by a straight staircase based on a circular arch. From the Golden Foot, the wall lead to the north-east, encircling the part of the nunnery closed to strangers (seclusion) and then turned sharply to the east, to meet Margrethe's wall by Lai Street. This section of the wall lost its importance later on and was either demolished or used to construct the stone walls of the nunnery.

The other section of the wall that Kanne ordered to be built had to link the fortress of Toompea and the southern defences of the lower town. The wall had to begin ' ... by the corner or horn of the greater castle' and be prolonged till the wooden gate by the Short Hill (pro Short Leg) in the lower town. This gate was called the seclusion of the town, but it was also popularly known as the outer ward (*clausura civitatis, vulgariter cyngele*). Since the commissions were very specific, prescribing the height of the walls etc., they were also carried out exactly as ordered. The no-man-land was thus closed, both routes linking the lower town with Toompea (Short Leg and Long Leg) were now sheltered by town walls. The main entrance to the fortress was at the side closest to Tõnismägi, as mentioned before.

Besides specific orders, Kanne also made several suggestions concerning the construction of fortifications. In the 1st half of the 14th century, spontaneous building outside the aldermanic city seems to have been widely spread. Major growth of the city occurred between 1335 and 1355. In the north, the guild city with Oleviste and Old Russian churches was united with the heart of the city. In the south, the city grew on the line between Niguliste church and St. Catherine's monastery. The area of the city almost doubled, there was a rapid growth in the number of residents. The functions of the city grew in accordance with the population growth, all institutions regulating the life of the city were reorganised. The Town Hall Square (Raekoja plats) became the new market place (*forum, Neue Markt*), a town hall (*consistorio, rathus*) was built (predecessor of the present Town Hall). Pikk Street (*longa rega, lange strate*) became the main street, guilds were granted building lots there. Innovations were made also outside the heart of the city, for example in the port, which was transferred to the cape in the north-east. Major works in the port have been recorded in 1336.

In 1335 or so, following Kanne's suggestion, the building of a **new town wall in the north and the south of the city** was started. It lasted a couple of decades, and brought about a complete change in the fortifications of the lower town. Works were probably strarted in the guild town, where simple walls with **wooden defence galleries** were built. Four differently built sections of the wall are known, all of them 1.1— 1.3 m thick at the ground level, height 4.35—5.6 m, some with loop-

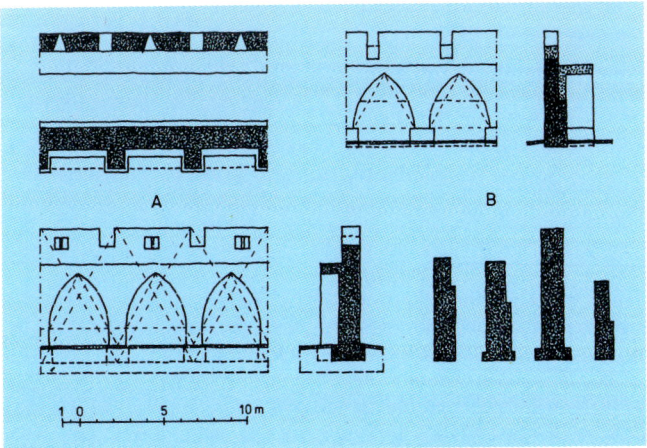

The outer side of the town wall near the Rope Hill Tower, where the wall sections built in 1335—1355 and 1360—1370 meet

Profiles of the town wall 1310—1355. A — wall with arched niches at the aldermanic town, B — different wall profiles at the guild town

holes, some without. This inicates that the walls were built by at least four organisations using their own masters and techniques. These organisations were most probably guilds and, according to a record from 1310, the King's vassals, who owned some plots of land by Lai Street (then called Nun Street = *platea sancti monialum*).

The northen wall was made up of straight sections. It began by the nunnery in the west, continuing in a long straight line until the site of the **Renten Tower**, then turned to the east, continuing to the site of the later **Stolting corner tower** and after that turned to the south, joining Margrethe's wall near the monasteries. There were two new gates in the wall front — **the Great and the Small Coast Gate.** Outside the north-western or the northern wall there was no moat.

The process of the construction of the town wall **on the southern side of the aldermanic town** was quite different. **A moat** was dug first. To fill it with water, King Waldemar IV permitted to take water from ' ...the Oxhead River, its springs and other places convenient for the purpose'. Construction of mills was also allowed. It is known that a 4 km derivation canal was built between the upper course of the Härjapea /Oxhead River and the town. Water flow in the canal could be controlled and it branched into a 1.5 km moat with a **cascade of watermills** on the southern, south-eastern and eastern side of the town. Harju, Karja and Viru watermills were situated by the corresponding gates, at that time they were called (starting from the upper one) '*de superiori-, de medio-, de infimo molendino*'. The construction of the mills between 1346 and 1349 was a joint venture of the town council and the citizens. At the end of the century, the town took the mills over one by one. Joint projects between the council and the citizens, including those involving building of walls and towers, were common in medieval cities.

Soon, however, most fortification works ceased or changed their nature, due to the St. George's Night Uprising by Estonians which began on April 23, 1343 and continued until 1345. Although Tallinn was never taken and the final victory was thus never achieved, Estonians acquired a reputation of a stubborn and tough nation, that followed them throughout the centuries to come. Estonians did achieve something, though: Denmark, which had ruled Estonia ruthlessly, sold its properties in the country to the Teutonic Order in 1346. The latter, in its turn, sold them to the Livonian Order in 1347.

1346—1561: II ORDER ERA

The new power sped up the fortification works in Tallinn, including completing the walls and towers of the lower town. The Order had its own ideas about how the works should be carried out. Apart from the aforementioned moat and the mill system, the **first wall with arched niches** was completed at the southern and south-eastern side of the town. First the earth dug out from the moat was piled up to even the land and form a 1—1.5 m high earth wall at the side of the moat closer to the town. A 1 m thick limestone plinth was buried in the earthworks

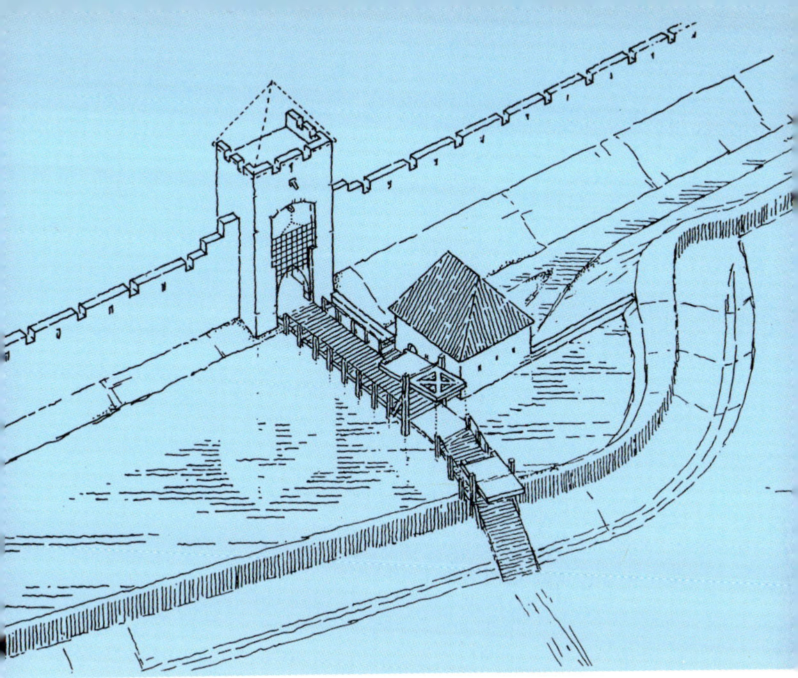

I Viru Gate with pond and water mill, built in 1345—1355 (reconstruction)

Restored and reinforced town wall between the Viru Gate and Helleman Tower. The arched niches date from 1335—1355, the defence gallery in the upper part probably from 1494—1497

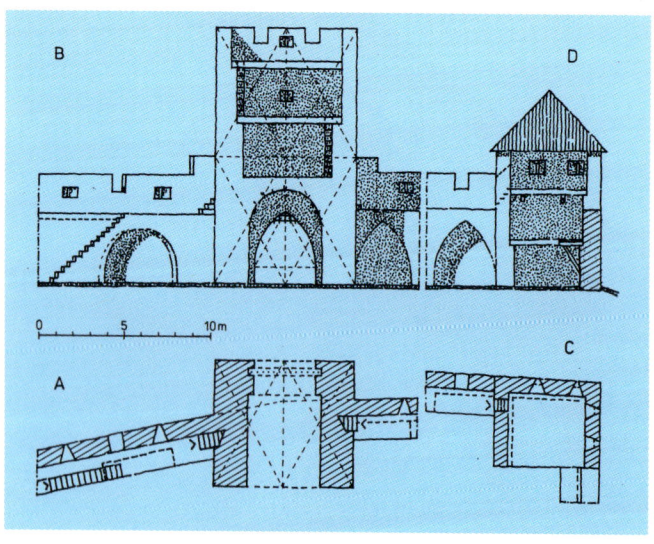

Arched niches on Müürivahe Street, built on the inner side of the older wall in the 1370s

Some fortifications of Tallinn, 1345—1355. A — the ground floor of the Great Coast Gate, B — view of the gate tower from the town, C — defence floor of the I Stolting Tower, D — view of the same tower from the town

on a layer of sand, to form a base for the new town wall. The 6.7 m high and 2.3—2.5 m thick wall was based on arched niches and had loopholes and a defence gallery. The breastwork of the gallery had loopholes of two different shapes in it — with parallel and narrowing sides. The shape of the arched niches was derived from an equilateral triangle; a regular hexagram seems to have been the basis for the general proportions.

The wall near the monastic land was probably built at the expense of the monks, as proven by the King's reminder on taxes from 1345. **The monks' wall** was 1 m lower than the sections built by aldermen (height 5.6 m, width 1.25 m) and had no arched niches.

By 1355, the fortifications were developed well enough to appoint chiefs and provide equipment for the towers and walls. The following is a short survey of works completed by the time.

1.6 km of new town wall had been built between 1335 and 1355. Five gate towers were built in the wall front. Although they differed from each other in size and details, they were all built according to the same system, that of the I Nun Gate. The **I Great Coast Gate** (*porta littoris, grote strantporte,* finally *Grosse Strandpforte*) had four storeys, probably due to the necessity of keeping watch over the coast and the port in the tower. The Great Coast Gate measured 8.4 by 7.2 m, and was 14.4 m high. The tower had a favourable location, 27 m above the sea level. Blueprints prove that the 3.5 m wide portal of the gate level was easily shut tight from the inside with strong doors and a log bolt, and from the outside, with a portcullis. Like in the I Kuldjala /Golden Foot Tower, an open stone staircase, supported by an arch, led to the first floor.

The **I Small Coast Gate** (*lutteke strantporte,* finally *Kleine Strandpforte*), originally named the Sand Gate (*porta sant, porta arena*) had a similar layout, but it was built at a sharper angle in relation to the walls. The exact measurements of the building are not known. The gate was demolished quite early and is mainly known thanks to several old town maps. From these, it is possible to conclude, however, that the Small Coast Gate was quite similar to the other gates built around that time. The entrance to the first floor of the tower was on the left (northern) side.

Then followed **Viru Gate**, in other languages always known as the Clay Gate (*porta argille, leimporte,* finally *Lehmpforte*). The street starting from the gate was also named Savi /Clay Street (*leymstrate, Lehmstrasse*). The names of Viru Gate and Viru Street are of Estonian origin and have been in use since the 19th century, but maybe even earlier. The gate tower has not been preserved, but old drawings and archaeological excavations have proven that the **I Viru Gate**, which was situated in line with the town wall in Viru Street was similar to the gates described above. The gate tower was 3-storied (measuring 8.4 by 7.2 m, height 14.6 m). There was a pond beyond the gate and around a mill. As the mill was built quite low in relation to the sea level, the wheel was fed from below. To raise the water level, the whole complex was surrounded by poles and earthworks strenghtened with clay.

The **original Cattle Gate** (8.4 by 7.2 m, height 14.3 m) was probably also 3-storied. The architecture and the location of the gate and the watermill greatly resembles that of the I Viru Gate. Analysis of the landscape shows that the water wheel in the mill could be driven either from above or from below. The Cattle Gate was first mentioned in 1365 as *porta pecorum, veporte*, but three years later already a name derived from the Estonian language — *porta karie* — was used, which later led to the name Karjavärav /Cattle Gate (*Karripforte*). The cattle of the aldermanic town was lead to the pastures (*veedrift*) by the gate, nearby was the Cattle Spring, where the cattle used to be watered.

The third gate in the new wall was **Harju Gate**, which in the Middle Ages and even later was called Sepa /Blacksmith's Gate (*porta fabrorum, smedeporte*, finally *Schmiedepforte*). The name of the gate which is used now was derived from Estonian (as in Viru Gate) and indicates that the road which started from the gate, led to Harju county. This tower was a little different from the others built at the same time. It was probably 3-storied (7.8 by 9.9 m). There was a mill with an above-fed water wheel and a pond outside the gate. The derivation canal ended in the pond and the cascade of mills also started from here. Harju pond was 12—15 metres above the sea level.

Between 1311 and 1355, six new stone gate towers, including the Nun Gate tower, had been completed. In addition to those, there was a wooden **gate by the Short Hill** (*singhele sub breve monte*), which at that time was an outer gate, locatied in the area of Rüütli Street. The wall by the so-called Danish King's Garden had not been built yet, the road to the gate began from Tõnismägi and continued via the present Rüütli /Knight Street. Another wooden **gate** was **under the Long Hill** (*phala sub longo monte*), but it was used as an inner gate between the lower town and Toompea, according to Kanne's regulations.

Plan analysis and tower chief lists prove that four corner towers were built between 1335 and 1355. The first among them was the **I Renten Tower**, which was erected at the meeting point of the new north-western and northern walls. The tower has been destroyed, but old drawings show that it was projecting and horse-shoe shaped ($\varnothing$ 10.2 m). The original height is not known. The **I Hinke Tower** was quite similar, it was built at the meeting point of the new south-eastern and eastern walls ($\varnothing$ 10.4 m). The building has been preserved in a reconstructed form, but no profound research has been carried out.

Two smaller corner towers were built as well. The **original Stolting Tower** (name of later origin) was built in a corner of the walls, thus not projecting. Research has proved that the tower had three floors and was based on a trapezoid measuring 4.85 (5.15) by 6.2 m, height 7.7 m. The uppermost floor, which could be reached by a staircase starting from the northern wall, had five spanned loopholes. Another small and probably non-projecting tower was at the south-western corner of the wall. In 1355 it (like many others in the lower town) did not yet have a name. Fifty years later, it was named **Kitsetorn /Goat Tower** (*Tzegen thorn*), probably because there was a goat stable nearby. No closer data about the tower is available.

Harju Gate and the water-mill in 1863, before demolition. Reproduction of a watercolour by M. Villier. Estonian History Museum

We have now dealt with all the walls, towers and gates that existed at that time. The town had seven outer gateways and four corner towers, altogether 11 buildings, which have been recorded in 1355. As there were two more towers by the nunnery and a gate under the Long Hill, the number of wall and gate towers in the lower town reached to 14.

Construction of defences became more active again due to the military conflict between the Hanseatic cities and Denmark, during which King Waldemar IV seized and plundered Visby in 1361. Permanent watch was established in the towers facing the sea, a special watch and defence tower, named **Sadamatorn /Port Tower** (*port torn*) was erected in the port. Most of the formerly built wall sections were now reconstructed: new defence galleries, which were supported by stone arches, replaced the former wooden passages.

Two new sections of walls were coped to the lower town, one secluding a part of Mihkli /St. Michael's nunnery in the north-western part of the town, the other enclosed Rüütli Street and the region of the Work Yards (*Marstallberg*) in the south-western part of the town, west of Niguliste /St. Nicholas church.Thus the gate below the Short Hill became an intermediate gate similar to the one below the Long Hill. Rüütli Street lost its function as the outer communication road to Harju Street. Both copings were important defence erections for the town. They were surrounded by the town wall between 1360 and 1370. The defence galleries of the walls were based on arched niches. The walls

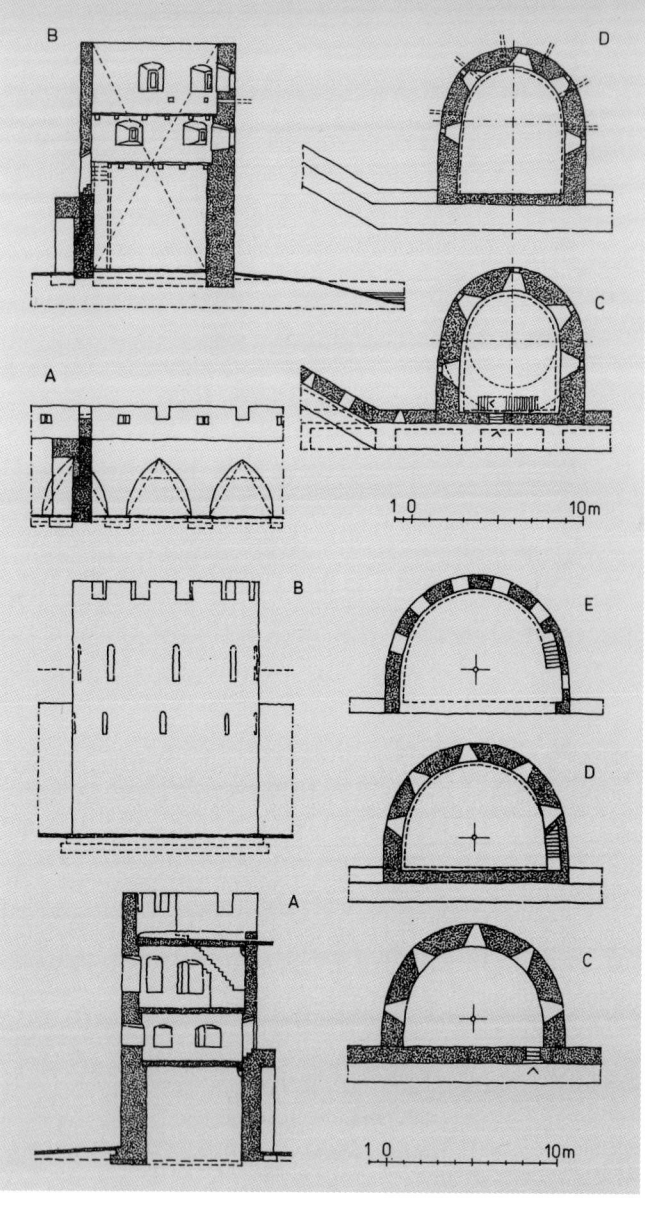

Some fortifications of Tallinn, approx. 1370. A — town wall with arched niches on the north-western side , B — elevation of the I Kõismäe /Rope Hill Tower, C — the lower defence floor of the same tower, D — the upper defence floor of the same tower
I Loewenschede Tower, built in 1371—1373. A — elevation of the tower, B — exterior, C...E — ground plans of defence floors

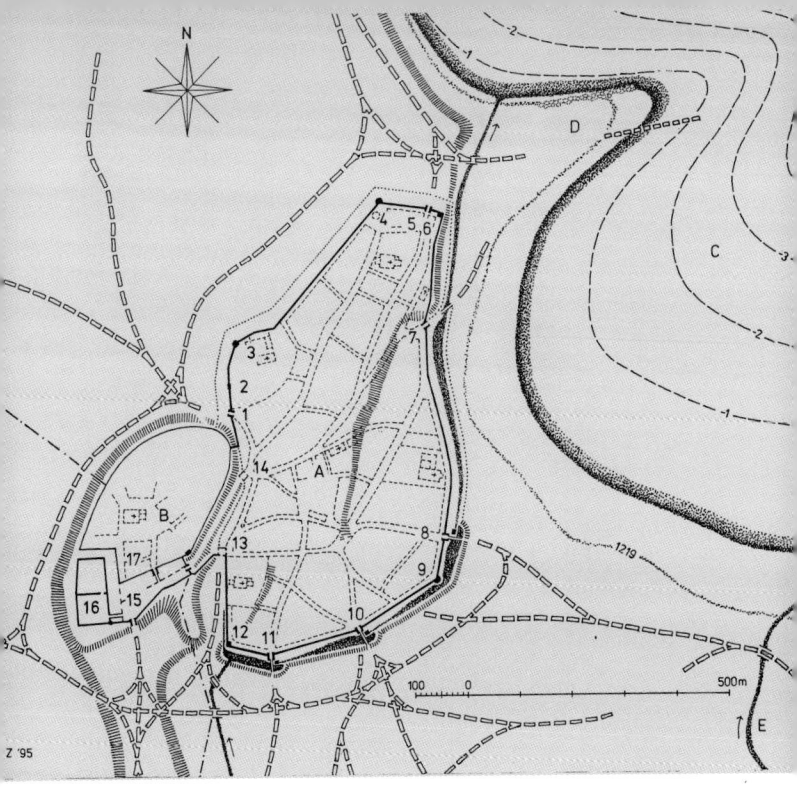

Topographical scheme of Tallinn, approx. 1355 (reconstruction). A — the lower town, B — Toompea, C — Tallinn Bay, D — the port, E — the Härjapea River, 1 — Nunnavärav /Nun Gate, 2 — Nunnatorn /Nun Tower, 3 — Kuldjala /Golden Foot Tower, 4 — Renten Tower, 5 — the Great Coast Gate, 6 — Stolting Tower, 7 — the Small Coast Gate, 8 — Viru Gate, 9 — Hinke Tower, 10 — Karja /Cattle Gate, 11 — Harju Gate, 12 — Kitsetorn /Goat Tower, 13 — gate below the Short Hill, 14 — gate below the Long Hill, 15 — outer ward of the castle, 16 — Order Castle, 17 — the Episcopal (Great) Castle

The border line between the lower town and the Order Castle, churches, cloisters, main roads, coast line and sea depth are shown.

were slightly thicker and higher than the ones built earlier, measuring 2.1—2.9 m in width and 7.0—8.1 m in height. **An outer ward** (*parcham*) was set up as well and so a double wall connected Harju Gate with the outer ward of the fortress. A **moat** was dug outside the northern and north-western walls. These works were completed by 1374.

Some defence towers were build in the wall front. Between 1370 and 1372, the town mayor Evert Kalle had rebuilt the *bastille*-like tower at the beginning of the north-western wall section on the St. Michael's nunnery ground into the three-storied **II Kuldjala /Golden Foot Tower** (13.1 m high), by adding two new defence floors. Both floors, separated by wooden inserted ceilings, had six loopholes, typical of the period. The rear side of the new tower was closed.

The outer side of the I Behind-the-Nuns Tower, built in 1372—1374, with supporting arches and loopholes

From here the wall continued to the place where the **Köismäe / Rope Hill Tower** was erected. It is interesting to note that the well-known horse-shoe-like ground design was used once again. The tower (⌀ 8.4 m, 13.3 m high) had three storeys, and two new defence floors with loopholes. The structure was closed from behind, and the second floor could be reached by the defence gallery through the portal. The Estonian name of the tower is a translation of the name it was given in the 16th century: *Thurm Reperbahn* (before: *achter der Repenbanen, Reper-Turm*, etc.); the name, in turn, came from the "Old Reperbahn" district near by, where rope and sail workshops — very important to Tallinn as a port — were situated.

Between Kuldjala and Köismäe there were three new towers. The first of them was a small oriel — **I Nunnadetagune /Behind-the-Nuns** (*arkenel achter den Nunnen*) tower, which was built between 1372 and 1374 by order of the town mayor Winend Louenschede. It had

*Megede Tower (Virgin Tower), founded in 1370—1373 and later built higher,
with the adjoining town wall and parcham-wall*

only one defence floor (5.6 by 3.2 m) which was supported by two
arched brackets from the outside and two pillars from the inside. The
tower has survived in a reconstructed form. Another similar tower, the
I Lippe Tower, which was situated between Köismäe and Loewenschede towers, and built between 1371 and 1373 by the later chief of
the tower Herman von Lippe, has unfortunately not survived, but we
know about it from old drawings.

From 1371 to 1373, Winend Loewenschede built a solid wall tower
between the saddle towers. The **I Loewenschede Tower** was four-storied, with a ground plan based on a projecting half-circle ($\varnothing$ 10.7 m,
height 14.7 m). The lower defence floors had narrow lintelled loopholes. The upper floor was an open parapetted defence platform, which
could lodge catapults, the heavy arms of the time. The tower had a fine
exterior, staircases on the wall and wooden inserted ceilings. The 2nd
floor could be reached via the defence gallery of the town wall.

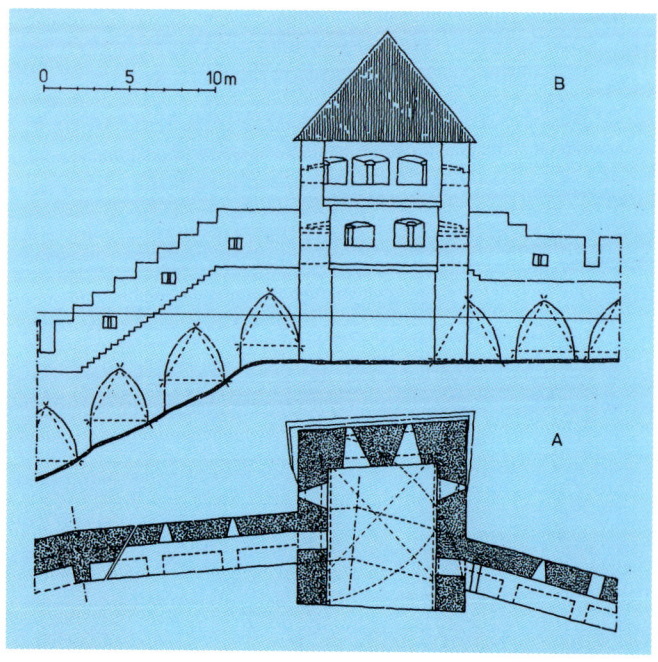

I Megede Tower, built in 1370—1373. A — lower defence floor, B — view from the town

The second **new section of the town wall** was built between the already existing Kitsetorn /Goat Tower and the corner of the outer ward of the great castle (... *cornu magni castri*). Between 1370 and 1373, a unique tower facing Tõnismägi was built in the middle of this section. The tower was based on a type widely used in Visby defences, which was somewhat out-dated for Tallinn. It was rectangular and opened at the rear. Due to its location at the steep edge of the Work Yards Hill (*Marstallberg*), the ground plan of the **I Megede Tower** was irregular (9.9 by (9.9+10.9) /2). It was 12.5 m high, two upper ones of its three floors were built for defence purposes. By 1373, the tower had acquired the name *Meghede torne*, which was probably derived from the name of Hinse Meghe, a citizen and *Bauherr* residing nearby. Its present name Neitsitorn /Virgin Tower, German *Mädchenturm*, which has been widely used since 1884, is based on an erroneous interpretation.

Other works were also carried out at about the same time. Alderman Arent van Renten had a former corner tower built higher, the tower with two new defence floors is known as the **II Renten Tower** (in 1410 recorded as *thorn Her Arnds van Renthen*). Between 1370 and 1372, alderman Tideman Eppinc (Epping) had another 3-storey tower built in the middle of the wall section leading to Köismäe Tower, south

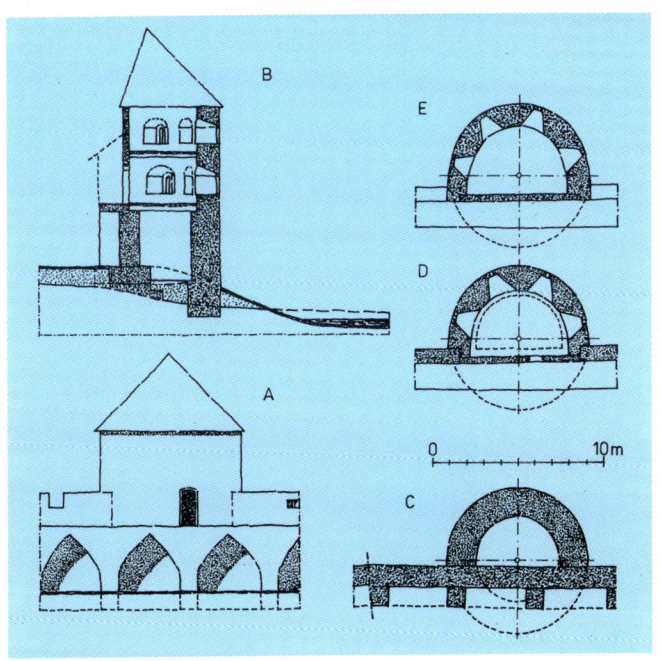

I Munkadetagune /Behind-the-Monks Tower, built around 1370. A —view from the town, B — elevation, C...E — ground plans of floors

of Renten Tower. The agreed name of the building, which in many aspects was similar to Köismäe Tower, can be the **I Epping Tower** (∅ 8.8 m, height 11.0 m). Later on, it has also been called 'the tower behind Oleviste parish' (*thorn achter sunte Olaues wedeme*).Both defence floors of the tower had five loopholes which were suitable for arbalests (*arborst*). It is known that the digging of a new moat was started by alderman Epping in the 1370s. He received funding both for defensive buildings (*ad fossatum*) and for digging the moat (*dat canal to makende*). Some works were carried out also at the nunnery (1371—1372), including the construction of the **I Sauna Tower**, a saddle tower with one defence floor (6.3 by 3.8 m, height 8.0 m). The name of the tower is conventional, reminding of a sauna nearby which belonged to the nuns and later caused a major conflict between the convent and the city.

Some building work was also done in the eastern side of the town. The **II Stolting Tower** was probably built around that time. A stone wall was added to the side facing the town. A three-storey semicircular tower named the **I Munkadetagune /Behind-the-Monks Tower** was built (∅ 8.4 m, height 9.0 m). The **monks' wall** nearby got arched niches. Both the wall and the tower are rather poorly built, which sug-

29

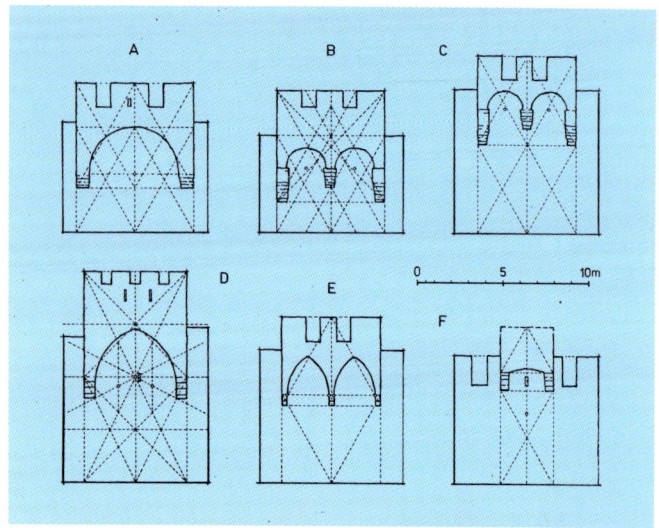

Some saddle towers of Tallinn and Visby. A — the I Nunnatorn /Nun Tower, B — the I Sauna Tower, C — the I Nunnadetagune /Behind-the-Nuns Tower, D — example of a saddle tower from Visby, E — a typical saddle tower of the Great Castle of Toompea, F — Talli Tower

gests that the works were funded by monks. Their master builders were probably the same ones who reconstructed the II Golden Foot Tower and erected the I Sauna Tower.

The second known list of tower chiefs and their military equipment dates from 1373. This document lists 15 towers with two chiefs for each one. The town wall actually had 20 towers at that time — 6 gate towers, 7 round towers, 2 rectangular towers and 5 saddle towers. The lower town also had two gates leading to Toompea, and Sadamatorn / Port Tower in the port. Although the new towers looked different, they were mostly constructed according to the same principles and using the same details. All of them were closed from behind, had inserted log ceilings supported by borders of the walls, and loopholes spanned by arches or lintels. The towers had either two or three defence floors, which were between 9 and 14.6 m in height. Walls were laid of thin limestone, were 1.5—1.8 m thick at the ground floor level and grew gradually thinner at the level of each new floor. The town wall was equally strong in most sections. Everywhere except in the vicinity of the nunnery, defence galleries were based on arched niches. **A moat and a palisade** now surrounded also the northern and north-western sides of the town. A logical development following the erection of this basic outer ward structure was the construction of the **first foregates**. These were narrow passages through the outer ward that had gates at both ends.

Long Leg Gate, built in 1380. View from the Long Leg

The techniques and typology of building prove that the late 14th and early 15th century architecture of Tallinn was characterized by an original usage of natural stone in Gothic buildings. Local master builders emerged who mastered the possibilities offered by local construction materials, including the combination of wood and stone. The buildings in the defence line were step by step adjusted for firearms, first and foremost cannons, which became widely spread from the 14th century onwards. Their precision improved and their destruction power was unparalleled, wiping away a strong wall or even an entire fortress.

Building continued. In 1380, the Livonian Order authorised the erection of a stone gate at the **Long Leg**. The **first gate tower** (a trapezoid measuring 6.2 by 6.8 m, height 11.6 m, three floors) was built. The gateway could be shut with strong doors and a log bolt from the lower town. Additional protection was provided by a portcullis hidden in the wall. The wooden Short Leg Gate was still below the hill. Three

Assauwe Tower on Müürivahe Street

new semicircular towers were built on the side of the town facing
the sea (∅ 8.4—8.8 m), evidently following the pattern of the formerly erected Munkadetagune /Behind-the-Monks Tower. The first
of them, the **I Wulfarditagune /Behind-Wulfard Tower** (*thorn achter
Wulfarde*) was completed somewhere between 1370 and 1390, and got
its name from a citizen residing nearby, Wulfard Rosendal from Åbo,
who till 1414 was also a tower chief. The next tower to be built was the
I Hattorpe-tagune /Behind-Hattorpe Tower (*thorn achter Hattorpe*),
which was located on the eastern side of the town and got its name
from the houses of Hattorpe. In the very vicinity, the **I Vene kiriku
tagune torn /Tower Behind the Russian Church** (*thorn by (achter)
der russ(is)schen kerken*) was erected. This tower was named after the
old Russian church, which in the 14th century was still located at
Olevimägi, but at the begining of the 15th century it was transferred to

Behind-the-Monks Tower on Müürivahe Street

Vene /Russian Street. The exact measurements of these towers are not known.

A couple of other new and different towers are known as well. A projecting three-storied **I Assauwe Tower** (∅ 9.6 m, height approx. 11 m) was built between Karja /Cattle and Harju gates. The Estonianised name of the tower (*Assauwen thorn*) was probably derived either from the name of the town's herdsman Asso or his yard (*Asso õu*). The **III Kitsetorn /Goat Tower** (1414 *Tzegen thorn*) was transferred to a new location at the corner of Rüütli and Müürivahe Streets (ground plan 9.2 by 8.7 m, destroyed). The **I Tallitorn /Talli Tower** (*Marstallthurm*, ground plan 3.1 by 3.1 m, one floor) was built at the Work Yard Hill between Megede Tower and the first gate of the fortress. The Order probably did not allow to construct a bigger tower near the fortress of Toompea. Tallitorn did not have a chief.

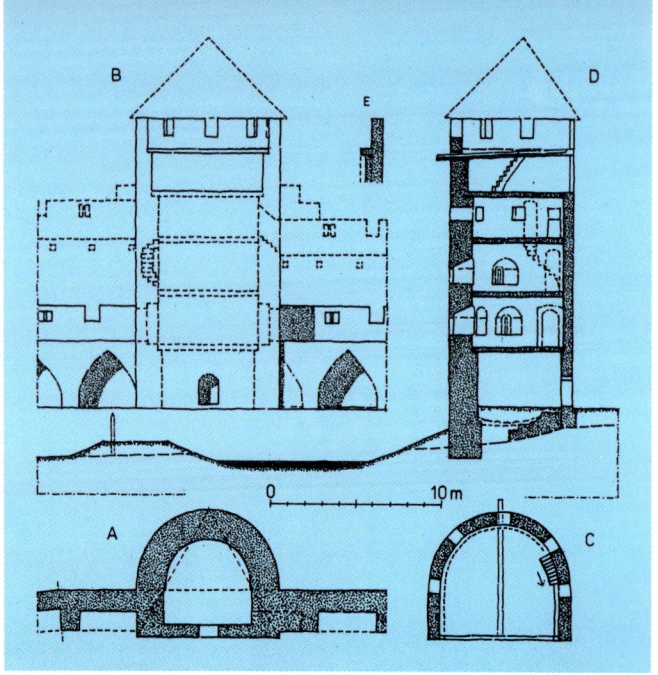

II Munkadetagune /Behind-the-Monks Tower, built at the end of the 14th century, A —ground floor, B —view from town, C — the upper defence floor (platform), D — elevation of the tower and the moat

The towers in the vicinity of Mihkli /St. Michael's convent were built higher, both the **II Sauna Tower** and the **II Nun Tower** got one more floor (average height of the towers now reached 9 m).

Some radical changes occurred soon. Intensive adjustment of Tallinn town wall for firearms had begun. To begin with, all defences were built higher, providing a better view of the activities of the enemy and extending the scope of arms of the defenders. The **II Epping Tower** got two more floors, thus becoming the first known high defence tower in the lower town of Tallinn. This building (height 17 m, 4 defence floors) now had five floors with wooden inserted ceilings, on the top of the tower there was an open platform where catapults could be set up.

Another similar building was the **II Munkadetagune /Behind-the-Monks Tower**, which now had 6 floors (2 for stores, 4 for defence purposes, height 16.5 m). The peculiarity of the tower is in the location of ammunition stores on the 1st and on the 5th floor. On the top of the tower, there was an open crenelated platform. Both the platform and the store under it were open at the side facing the town, the upper stories could be reached via a turreted staircase. At the beginning the tower could be reached from the town wall from both sides, but later, when the wall was built higher, only from the southern side.

The third of the new towers is the **I Kuraditorn /Devil Tower**, which has also been named Kuradiema /Devil's Mother or Kuradi-

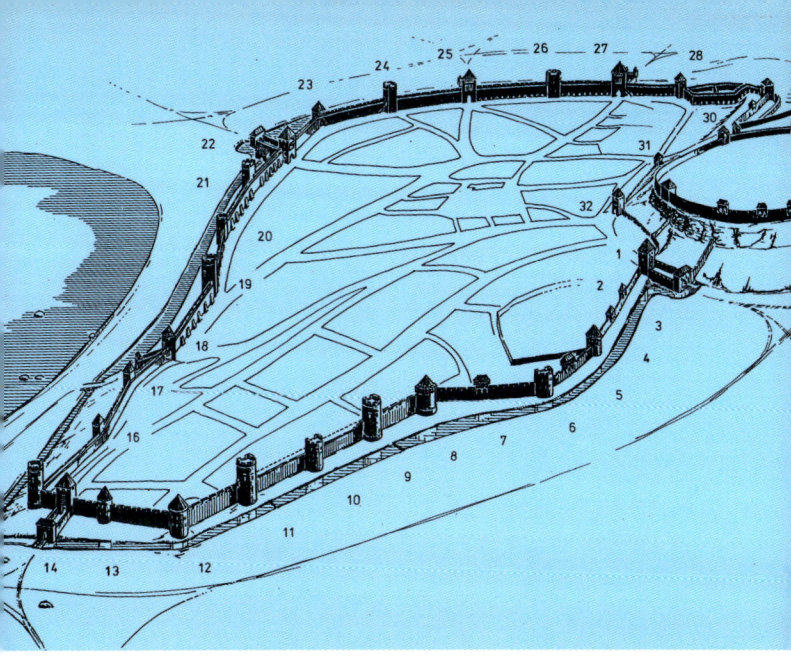

The fortifications of the lower town of Tallinn, 1410—1414 (reconstruction). 1 — Nunnavärav /Nun Gate, 2 — Nunnatorn /Nun Tower, 3 — Sauna Tower, 4 — Kuldjala /Golden Foot Tower, 5 — Nunnadetagune /Behind-the-Nuns Tower, 6 — Loewenschede Tower, 7 — Lippe Tower, 8 — Köismäe /Rope Hill Tower, 9 — Plate Tower, 10 — Epping Tower, 11 — Grusbeke-tagune /Behind-Grusbeke Tower, 12 —Renten Tower, 13 — Wulfardi-tagune /Behind-Wulfard Tower, 14 — Great Coast Gate, 15 — Stolting Tower, 16 — Hattorpe-tagune /Behind-Hattorpe Tower, 17 — tower by the old Russian church, 18 — Small Coast Gate, 19 — Bremen Tower, 20 — Munkadetagune /Behind-the-Monks Tower, 21 — Helleman Tower, 22 — Viru Gate, 23 — Hinke Tower, 24 — Kuraditorn /Devil Tower, 25 — Karja /Cattle Gate, 26 — Assauwe Tower, 27 — Harju Gate, 28 — Kitsetorn /Goat Tower, 29 — Megede Tower, 30 — Talli Tower, 31 — gate below the Short Hill, 32 — Long Leg Gate

vanaema /Devil's Grandmother Tower (*Duuels thorn, Duvelsmoder, Teuffelsthurm, Teuffels-Grossmutter* etc). The building was situated between Hinke Tower and Karja /Cattle Gate, in line with the present Väike-Karja Street. The name of the tower was probably derived from the name of a nearby estate owner, Johannes Düvelsmoder (also, *Düvel, Grimmedüvel, Grimme*). The building has not been preserved, but research and 1728/38 survey charts lead us to believe that it was also one of the first high towers. The tower (∅ 9.6 m, height 19.2 m) had four storeys with wooden inserted ceilings, supported by borders. The walls grew thinner towards upper floors. Later the ceilings were supported by vaults.

The three described towers were a transition to a completely new type of high towers in Tallinn. In late 14th and early 15th century, six new towers were erected. Their ground plans were based on three quarters of a circle. Some were completely new buildings, some major re-

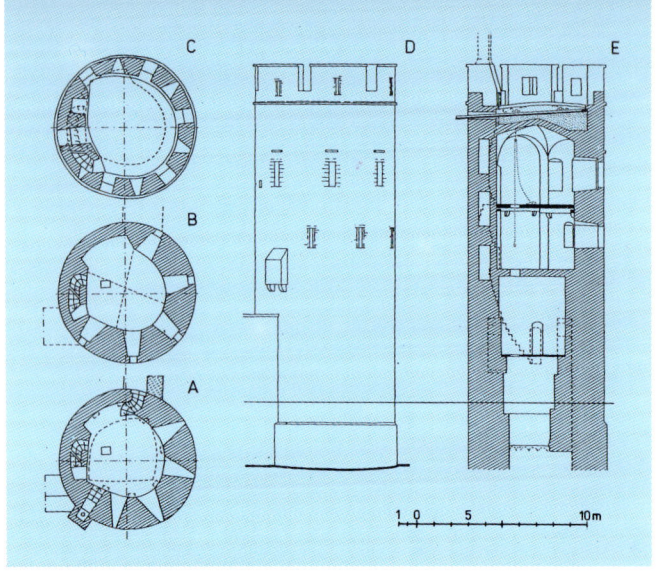

III Stolting Tower, built at the beginning of the 15th century. A...C — ground plans of defence floors, D — view from the east, E — elevation

constructions. They had extremely thick walls (sides of the lower part 1.9—2.5 m, front 2.8—3.0 m) supposed to withstand both catapults and firearms. The upper parts of the towers were meant for new types of defences, while the lower parts had a completely different function. These towers were the **III Stolting Tower,** the **II Bremen Tower,** the **I Helleman Tower,** the **I Plate Tower,** the **I Grusbeke-tagune /Behind-Grusbeke Tower** and the **II Hinke Tower.** The reconstructed III Stolting Tower had three defence floors, unlike most of the other new towers of the time, which typically had two. The lower defence floor usually had a vaulted ceiling and was meant for firearms, the upper one was an open platform with a water-tight floor, typically crenelated parapet, meant for setting up projectiles (ballistae, catapults). These 21.5— 24 m high towers, typical of the peak in the development of vertical defence, probably followed the example of **Pikk /Tall Hermann,** the new south-western corner tower of the Toompea Order Castle (*Lange Herman,* built in 1370, ∅ 9.65 m, height approx. 35 m). Most of the towers built or rebuilt in the lower town in the 15th century, in their turn, were based on the architecture of those new towers.

The introduction of new type of buildings, which were adjusted for firearms, also brought about a decisive fortification of the town wall. Arched niches, which had previously made the walls relatively weak, were filled, potentially weak sections were supported by buttresses, walls were built higher and equipped with a new parapet. As the small-arms were relatively long, slow to use and could not be exposed to water, the defence gallery was extended by means of wooden brackets or cantilevers, and the entire gallery was covered by a roof. The height of the **buttressed walls** reached to 13 m. Some sections of the wall,

III Stolting Tower, built in the beginning of the 15th century

like the one in the vicinity of the nunnery, for example, were still low (7—9 m) weak walls with wooden defence galleries, but even there, the gallery was now roofed.

The third known list of tower chiefs dates from 1410—1414. It includes 27 towers. Research proves, however, that the city actually had 32 towers and gates at the time. From 1373, nine new towers had been built and at least ten rebuilt. Approximately 60 per cent of the town wall had been secured thoroughly and about 30 per cent to some extent. These major developments will be outlined below.

The first among the new high towers was probably the **III Stolting Tower**, originally a small rectangular building, which was reconstruct-

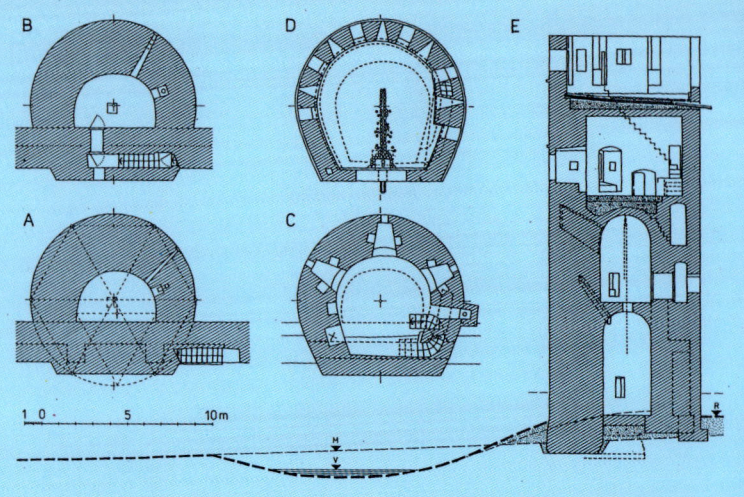

I Bremen Tower, built at the beginning of the 15th century. A...D — ground plans of different floors, E — elevation of the tower and the moat, M — profile of the ground before the tower was built, R — profile of the ground after the tower was built, V — water level in the moat

ed into a 5-storey thin open roundel with an exceptional circular ground plan (Ø 8.0 m, height 22.8 m). The lower part of the tower, which was covered by a barrel vault, held two storage floors. These floors could be reached via a portal at the level of the first floor. Steps led to the first defence floor from the same portal. After entering, four loopholes narrowing into slits could be seen in the outer perimeter. Next to the steps, there was a latrine niche with a floor descending gradually to a stone bench and a "toilet seat". From the outside, the latrine turreted out of the wall in a shape of a typical *dansker*. It was supported by stone brackets at the junction of the wall and the tower in a manner similar to that used in the Tall Hermann. This layout became traditional in the wall towers of Tallinn, except in smaller saddle towers. From there, the steps wound to the second defence floor, which had five newly shaped hatched firing chambers. The room originally had a wooden inserted ceiling, that was replaced by a cross-vault in the 15th century. The upper floor was an open, crenelated platform. The floor was water-tight, with a gutter in the middle which led the rain water to the spout. Above the steps, where the wall was thicker, there was a fireplace. This became a tradition in Tallinn as well. In peace time, the tower was covered with a roof, topped by a weather vane. On the platform of the Stolting Tower, 35 meters from the sea level, there was a permanent coast guard. The name of the tower (1414 *Stoltynk*) is probably derived from the name of a citizen, Nicolaus Stolthing, who also was most probably in charge of building (*Bauherr*).

The name of the **II Bremen** (*Bremer*) **Tower** was derived from the name of a citizen Hinze van Bremen who lived opposite the tower in

Bremen Tower, built in the beginning of the 15th century

the 1370s. At this time, there probably was a small saddle tower in this place in the town wall. Between 1400 and 1410, a 4-storied, multifunctional tower (∅ 9.7 m, outer wall 3.0 m at the ground level, height 21.6 m) replaced the original one. The two lower floors were used as a roundhouse (1452 *Bremen de vangen torne*), that could be reached by a special staircase from the street. The oak doors braced with iron were on the 2nd floor, from where it was possible to descend to the lower dungeon through a hatch. The vaulted rooms had mured floors, and there were latrine niches and narrow barred windows in the walls. The upper part of the tower had two defence floors, typical of the period: a room with a *dansker* (projecting latrine), three cannon chambers and a fireplace below, and a big open crenelated platform above. The cobbled

Outer door of the Bremen Tower roundhouse
The inner oak door on the 1 st floor of the roundhouse in the lower part of the
Bremen Tower
Latrine niche in the 1 st floor wall of the Bremen Tower roundhouse

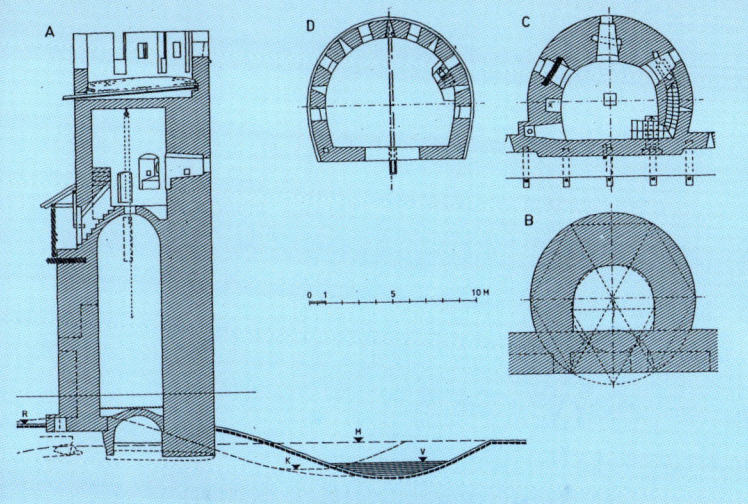

1 Hellemann Tower, built at the beginning of the 15th century. A — elevation of the tower and the moat, B...D — ground plans of floors, K — profile of the original moat, M — original ground profile, R — profile of the ground after widening the moat, V — water level in the moat

and clay-tightened floor of the latter has been preserved and was restored between 1957 and 1959.

The **1 Helleman Tower** was named upon its foundation at the beginning of the 15th century, probably after a citizen who lived nearby (*Helle, Holleman*). The tower was open (Ø 9.65 m, height 22.0 m). There was a 11 m high vaulted ammunition store in the lower part of the tower and two defence floors in the upper part. The lower defence floor could be reached by a staircase from the buttressed town wall. There was a latrine, a fireplace and three new type cannon chambers, where the cannons were based on strong log mounts (*lafette*) that were fixed to the wall. The loopholes (embrasures) were rounded, which suggests that large-calibre cannons were used. From the point of view of military technique, this solution was quite advanced. Ammunition could be lifted directly from the store below by means of a block mechanism. The uppermost floor that could be reached via a steep staircase was an open platform with 11 loopholes and an open rear part to facilitate transportation. The floor was water-tight and the whole construction was carried out following limestone building techniques, typical of Tallinn (*opus revalicum*). The tower that was located in a strategic position next to Viru Gate was evidently used until the Great Northern War (1700—1710).

The name of the **1 Plate Tower** is conventional and is based on the name of one of the tower chiefs mentioned in the record of 1410—1414 (*Herbord Plaete, Wenemar van der Beke*). The shape of the tower formed three-quarters of a barrel (Ø 9.75 m, height 23.9 m), the socle was projecting. In the lower part there was a merchandise (leather etc)

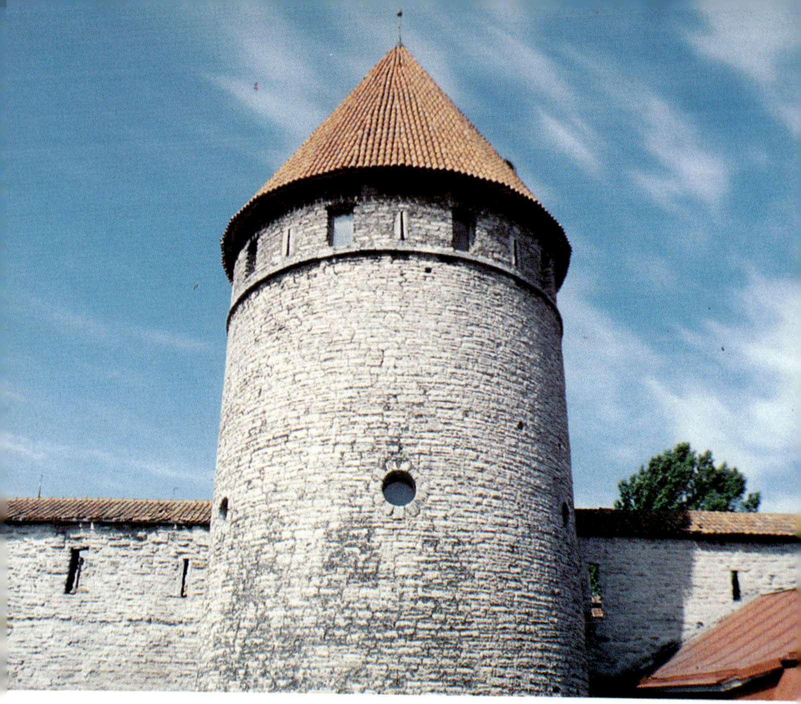

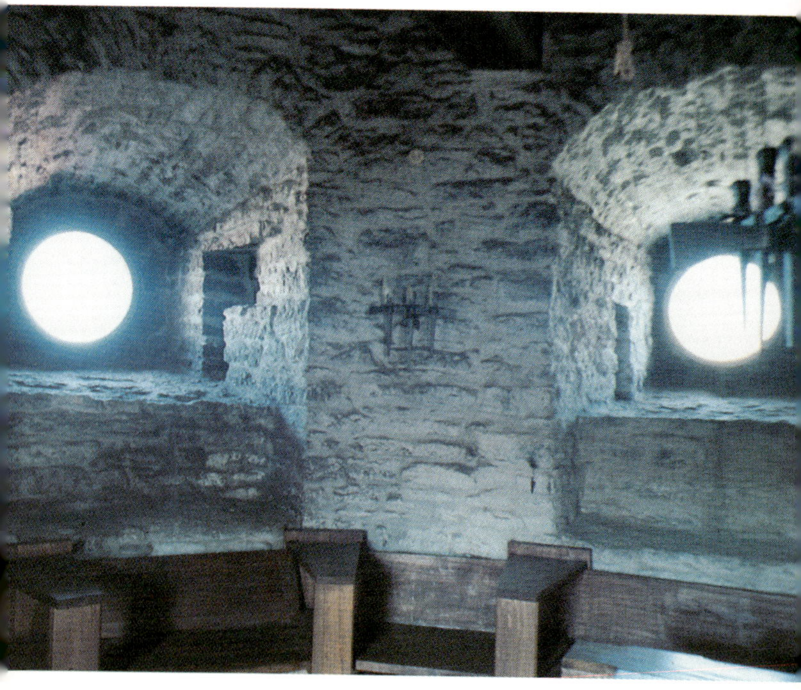

← *Helleman Tower, built in the beginning of the 15th century*
← *Embrasures of the Helleman Tower from the inside*
Helleman Tower is built using the beautiful opus revalicum *masony technique.*
Rounded opening of an embrasure from the outside
All high defence towers of Tallinn had projecting latrines (danskers) like Behind-Grusbeke Tower

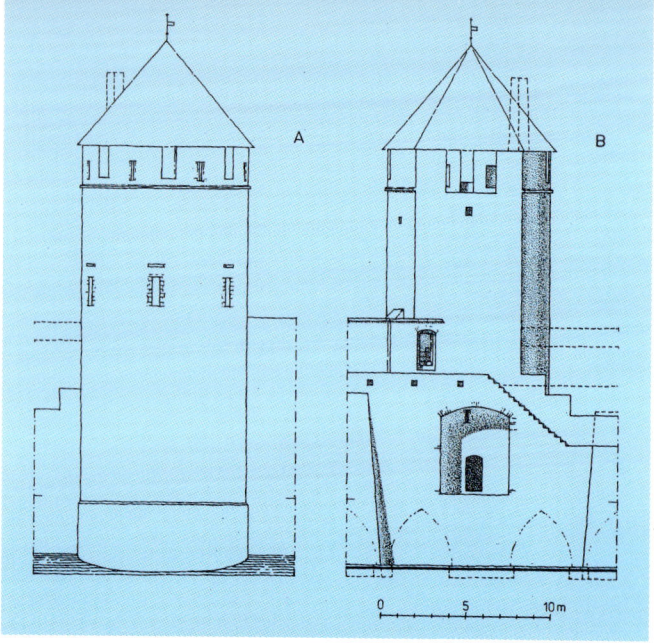

1 Plate Tower, built at the beginning of the 15th century. A — exterior, B —view from the town before the northern section of town wall was built higher

store. It was a 13-m high vaulted room, divided into two parts by an inserted ceiling. In the upper part, there was a narrow window, in the lower part, a door to Laboratooriumi Street. Both the window and the door were in bays in the wall above the ground level. Above them there was the partly renewed defence gallery of the town wall. Differences in the height of the town wall in neighbouring sections amounted to 4.6 m. From the southern buttressed wall, a door and a short staircase led to the lower defence floor. This room had three firing chambers with fixed log mounts and a fireplace. To proceed, one had to use a ladder to reach a wall staircase that started at 2.1 m from the ground — a known defence technique that was taken into use once again. The upper floor had a thick (1.4 m) parapet with 9 loopholes or slots. The rear of the tower was open to make lifting equipment possible, the floor was water-tight. During peace time, the tower was covered by a roof, topped by a gilded and colourful weather vane.

The lower section of the town wall north of Plate Tower ended by the **I Grusbeke-tagune /Behind-Grusbeke Tower**. From there, a buttressed wall continued to Renten Tower. The stairs leading from the lower part of the wall to the higher one were probably in the same place where they can be seen now. The tower was built in the middle of the wall section leading from Epping to Renten Tower. Its old name (1410—1414 *achter Grusbeken*) was derived from the name of a citizen, Arnd Grusbeke, who owned a house in the vicinity. Like Helle-mann and Plate towers, this one also had two parts and three stories (∅

44

9.65 m, ammunition store below and two defence floors above). The store was a 13 m high vaulted room with one door facing the town, one slot window in the side and a hatch in the ceiling. Of the two defence floors, only the lower one has been preserved. There were 3 firing chambers in its convex wall and a latrine (*dansker*) in the corner opposite the entrance. On the side facing the town, there was a light and transportation hole, which was somewhat exceptional. The original upper floor has been destroyed, since the tower had no roof for nearly 70 years. When it was finally restored in 1935—1936, the old walls were demolished to the floor level. The builders of the new upper floor unfortunately did not follow the original scheme. It is known, however, that in the 15th century, the upper defence floor was a platform with loopholes, fireplace and a water tight floor.

The **II Hinke Tower** was approximately twice the size of the first one. This defence building was much like Hellemann Tower: it had three storeys, 2.8 m thick walls and its height was 22 m from the street level. The lower part housed a 13 m high vaulted store with one door facing the town. There were two typical defence floors in the upper part. The lower one had four rounded firing chambers and probably a *dansker* near the entrance. There must have been a fireplace somewhere as well. The upper open defence floor which was destroyed at the end of the last century, had 11 typical loopholes. The upper part of the tower could be reached from the gallery of the heightened, strong town wall (height 10—11 m). Defenders had to climb a winding staircase which was built near the south-western corner of the tower at the same time the wall was made higher. There were 12 similar **staircases** and **special turrets** in the lower town, about half of them by the gates.

At the time the aforementioned buildings were finished, the so-called **old foregates** had been completed at the outer end of all lower town gateways. The outer ward was thus closed as well, either with a simple palisade or one on top of earthworks, with gates outside the moat. The defence of the ponds near Harju, Karja /Cattle and Viru gates was vital, since the fresh water of these ponds had become an important source of drinking water for the town. At the turn of the 14th and 15th century, the first wooden pipes that fed both public and private wells had been earthed. These works were supervised by Johannes Bonnynghof, a citizen of Tallinn and a water works expert, who had worked for the town since 1396. The ponds by the mills were also used to water horses (*perdedrenke*), unharnessed horses could be led to water through the areas between the gates. From the 15th century onwards, these places were cobbled and kept open also in winter time.

From the last quarter of the 14th century, extensive works were carried out to reconstruct and renovate the **whole defence zone**. During some periods, the works intensified due to the development of new military techniques, or complicated political situation at home or abroad. These situations escalated into military conflicts in the territory of Estonia, for example between 1396 and 1397, 1406 and 1409. Tallinn and northern Estonia were a territory of the Livonian Order (*Livländischer Orden*), so Tallinn, although a free city, was often carried along in the conflicts on the side of the Order. Another headache for Hanseatic Tallinn were the so-called Vitalian Brothers (*Vitalienbrüder*), well organised pirates who pirateered, plundered and sank ships in the Baltic Sea at the end of the 14th and beginning of the 15th century. They even managed to siege Gotland and its capital Visby in 1394, and also took part in the conflicts within Livonia. For the citizens of Tallinn, who could trust only their own forces, this brought about a necessity of being constantly alert and entailed great defence costs.

Despite all that, the economic life of Hanseatic Tallinn, including its architecture, was flourishing in the 15th century. The town had been given several privileges for foreign and domestic trade and this contributed much to the income of the city. As a result, there was much quality building going on. The formerly used vague Romanesque-Gothic style in architecture had developed into a well proportioned but modest Nordic Gothic tardif style, characterised by the use of natural stone and fine details. From 1348, the town stone pit was situated at Lasnamäe (*Lakesberg*), 3 km out of Tallinn. Up to 40 layers of hard slabs of Uhaku and Lasnamäe level limestone were cut there, the layers being 4—22 cm thick. Stone types were sorted in the pit, to maximise the use of different layers. Proceeding from the character of the stone, the cutters and masons created a special laying method, handling 2 or 3 rows of different-sized stones simultaneously. Using the Roman terminology, this technique could be called *opus revalicum*. It reminds a bit of the *opus mixtum* technique in mixed masonry, where a layer of natural stone was evened with bricks. Since Tallinn employed up to 30 master builders with their journeymen and apprentices at the same time, other systems were being used as well, for example *opus isodomum, opus pseudoisodomum, opus rusticum, opus quadratum.* Techniques known from *opus gallicum* were used to strengthen walls by timbers. All these techniques can be seen in the architecture of Tallinn from the 14th century on, *opus revalicum* was widely used in building the town wall and the towers.

Fortifications had to be continuously updated due to the rapid development of firearms. Firearms, that at the beginning were used mainly to scare horses, quickly developed into a range of different types of mobile and fixed cannons, rifles, shotguns, pistols, and hand grenades, varying in calibre and ignition systems. Mining was introduced. Since 1396, the town had its own cannon master, the first cannons were made in Tallinn at the turn of the century. Changes in fortification techniques were, of course, much slower. For a period of time, fortification systems contradicted each other. On one hand, vertical fortification was continued — towers and walls were built higher. On the other hand, horizontal fortification was introduced already in the 1370s — the defence zone was made deeper and extended further from the town wall. For these reasons, the development of the fortifications of Tallinn in the 15th century was extremely complicated.

The towers of the lower town mentioned in the 1410—1414 list differed in type and size, some sections of the town wall were high and strong, while others were quite low. One of the weakest sections was

Kuldjala /Golden Foot Tower building developments. A — II tower, built in 1370 —1372, B — upper part of the III Kuldjala /Golden Foot Tower and the hourding, built approx. 1422—1425 (reconstruction)

near Mihkli /St. Michael's convent where the defenders could not reach the wall. As the town did not reach an agreement with the nunnery, the magistracy decided to make a passageway between the wall and the cloister, demolishing the sauna and the granary of the nuns. This caused a major dispute between the magistracy and the convent, which in 1422 ended at a court session presided by the Order Master. The court ruled that the ownership of the wall and the towers be transferred from the nunnery to the city. The sauna and the granary were restored and the nunnery was freed from the obligation of building town walls. Soon after that, the wall in the vicinity of the nunnery was made up to 10 m high, a new wooden bracket-supported defence gallery was built.

Towers were reconstructed as well, creating thus the **III Nunnatorn /Nun Tower**, the **III Saunatorn /Sauna Tower** and the **III Kuldjala /Golden Foot Tower**. The first two got new faces towards the town and new upper floors (height 12.2 m from the ground). Kuldjala Tower got a new weather boarding, which strengthened the building considerably (walls 2.3—3.1 m thick at the ground level, height 13.5 m). An original projecting defence floor, called hourding, was added. It was made of timber and supported by brackets. That is where the final name of the tower originates from: in the list of 1410—1414, it was still called the "badly-roofed" (*quad dack*) tower, but in 1434, the name Kuldne jalg /Golden Foot (*de goldenevoet= de guldene Voet*) was recorded. The magistracy had paid for the building and the repairs (*to makende vnde to beterende*). It is documented that several people got paid for the building of the tower, and that works at Nunnavärav /Nun Gate

47

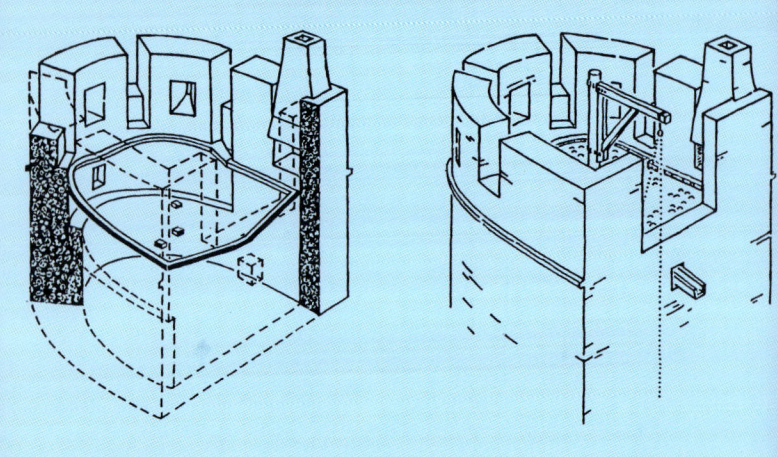

Upper part of the III Munkadetagune /Behind-the-Monks Tower, an open plat-form typical of Tallinn, built around 1438 (reconstruction)

were started around the same time, which leads us to believe that the whole section of the town wall between the Golden Foot Tower and the Nun Gate was reconstructed. Hourdings were probably built at the Nun Tower and the Sauna Tower as well.

Research has proven that the **II Köismäe /Rope Hill Tower** also got a hourding. The reconstruction was undertaken between 1436 and 1437 by alderman Michael Notiken, the tower was right behind his house (*achter sime huse*). A higher tower may have been planned, but for one reason or another, only the lower part was strengthened according to the same pattern used at the Golden Foot Tower (wall 2.4—3 m thick at the ground level). Besides that, a hourding was added. Hourdings were built because of the increasing use of gunpowder in military technique, especially the development of mining. The attackers often tried to reach the walls by using camouflaged trenches or tunnels, and it was easy to observe their "digging" from the projecting hourding and fight back, since it had loopholes also in the floor.

Tallinn suffered from a major fire in 1433. Among other buildings, the fire also destroyed the roofs of the Dominican Monastery, as well as the roof and the inserted ceilings of the Behind-the-Monks. The tower was reconstructed in 1438. The new six-floor building is known as the **III Behind-the-Monks Tower** (height 21.7 m, wooden inserted ceilings, two defence floors). The upper floor was an open platform with a water tight floor sloping gently (18 per cent) towards the centre. Water was drained out of the tower by means of a central gutter and a spout. There was a transportation hole at the rear, 4+3 loopholes in the parapet, and a fireplace with a chimney on the landing. The tower was built using the half-timbered construction technique typical of Tallinn. Once it was ready, its lower part held one of the arsenals of the city (*bussen laden*). The upper floor could be reached only from the wall south of the tower. It was possible to ascend to the wall by steps near Viru Gate. If one wished to mount to the wall north of the Behind-the-Monks, one had to use the winding stairs in a separate **turret** 8—10 m further off, which was set up at the same time with the buttresses of the town wall. The whole town wall was divided into similar sections, this improved the defence. Similar barrel-shaped turret with winding stairs, partly projecting from the wall, is known to have been built in the interior wall of the main tower at Karja /Cattle Gate.

According to the books of the magistracy, a number of buildings were reconstructed during the same period. These included the **Nun Gate** and the main **gateway** of the **Great Coast Gate**. The **II Loewenschede** and the **II Assauwe towers** were set up. Both gate towers have been destroyed, but it is probable that they were built two floors higher, like other towers rebuilt in the same period. Only small-scale recosntructions were carried out at **Loewenschede**, the sides and the rear were reinforced. The **II Assauwe Tower**, on the other hand, was radically rebuilt, making it similar to other high open towers of the period. The old town wall by the tower was demolished, and the new tower was based deep in the ground, probably because of the thick layer of peat under the former wall. The new tower was thus only 17.3 m from the street level, although the total height of its store and two defence floors amounted to 20 m. The town wall, although built higher, was also rather low, the gallery located at 9.8 m.The wall was not buttressed, and the passage connecting its sections led as a gallery through the rear part of the II Assauwe Tower. The gallery led to the lower defence floor, stairs from that level to the other floors.

Renovation of the gateways of the lower town was started as well. **Towers of the main gates** were built higher, and foregates, typical of the 15th century, were built. First of all, the **pond by Viru mill** was reconstructed from 1439 to 1445. Considering the location of the foregate, a new polygonal section of the ditch was dug. It was surrounded by earthworks topped with a palisade. Similar procedures were carried out at the **Nun Gate** from 1439—1445.

The next renovation was carried out at **Viru Gate**, where a new foregate (*de butenste Lemporte*) was built in two stages (1446—1447, 1453—1456). The side towers of the foregate have been preserved day. The main tower of Viru Gate, which was situated in line with the town wall in the middle of the present Viru Street, was built higher as well. The project was extensive, involving earthing of fresh water pipes which departed from the new mill-pond. The scale of the works is characterised by the fact that civil servants supervised the work of the carpenters and other workers and provided them with beer, dried fish, pork fat, fried hemp seed, etc. A new well was dug by the gate and the **watering place for horses** renewed. Research has proven that the former foregate house was widened and lengthened, it was closed by a 20 m wide and 15 m high gate wall, with one portal for horses and carriages and an-

49

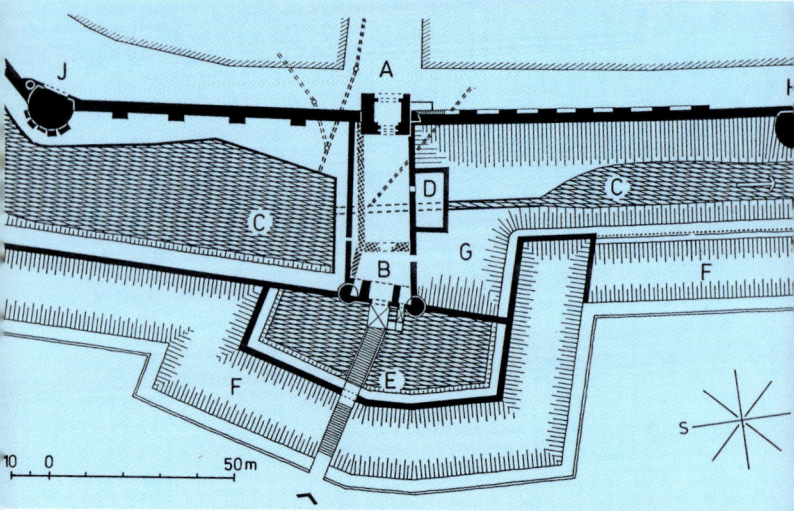

Viru Gate complex after the 2nd foregate was built in 1446—1456 (reconstruction). A — main gate, B — foregate, C — main moat and mill pond, D — Viru water mill, E — earthworks outside the foregate, F — outer moat, G — place for watering horses (perdedrenke), H — Hellemann Tower, J — Hinke Tower

other for pedestrians. There were loopholes in the wall and a *dansker* above the main portal, through which boiling water or tar could be cast on an enemy below. The chains of the drawbridge were also led through the holes there. The triangle lintelled recesses in the walls were probably decorated with coats-of-arms of the town and carved figures of saints. The main gate tower was five-storied, on the lower floors there were rooms for the guards and the portculis mechanism, and above them there were three defence floors.

The reconstruction of Viru Gate complex marked the beginning of the general modernisation of Tallinn's fortifications, which between 1454—1456 became so extensive that the town faced temporary financial difficulties. The direct cause of the fortifications was a war between Poland and the Teutonic Order, known as the 13-Year War (1454—1466). As a subject of the Order, Tallinn apparently took part in the conflict on its side. From 1448 to 1453, the **main tower of Harju Gate** was reconstructed (height approx. 21 m, 5 floors, the upper one a platform), besides the former foregate, the **2nd foregate complex** (gatehouse with two approx. 19-m side towers and a drawbridge), and a new polygonal moat with surrounding earthworks were built. The complex was one of the longest in Tallinn (approx. 55 m) and had three gates. The first gate led to the mill and the lock-gate, as well as the place then named 'place for watering horses outside the Blacksmith Gate' (*perdedrenke over buten der smedeporten*). The works were

Side towers of the second foregate of the Viru Gate, built in 1446—1456. The gate building between the towers was demolished in 1888

completed by 1452, when the towers of the gate complex got weather-vanes with gilded crosses and knobs. The table (*brett*) depicting the birth of Christ decorated a recess inside the main gate, three statues of St. Victor were set up on the foregate.

In 1448, the walls on the northern side of the town were built higher. Between 1434 and 1460, the **2nd foregate of the Great Coast Gate** complex was erected and the **main tower** was rebuilt. The architecture of the foregate complex is well recorded, and one of the foregate towers has been preserved. The new foregate, situated 39 m from the main gate, was 18.7 m wide in the front and consisted of a gatehouse and high-socled side towers. In the middle of the building there was a 3.4 m portal with strong double door and a drawbridge with levers and counterweights. Similar drawbridges were known in other locations in Estonia, such as Toompea castle and Padise monastery. Earthworks were adjacent to both sides of the foregate. The eastern side continued into a earlier built double wall near Stolting Tower, which went on until the next gate.

The next was the **Small Coast Gate**. From 1453 to 1456, the **main gate tower** was reconstructed and a **2nd foregate** was added to the complex. The **moat and the earthworks** on both sides of the gate were renovated between 1457 and 1460. The main gate got a new stone roof and a weather vane with a 'big knob' (*de grote knop vpp der Lutken Strantporten*) already in 1454, the foregate (*Lutke butenste strantporte*) soon after that. The only drawings of the gates are those on a city map and a maquette dating from 1683. The data available suggests that the main gate tower was like other analogous towers. The foregate must have had 2 floors, like Harju foregate.

Between 1452 and 1456, the **II Wulfarditagune /Behind-Wulfard Tower** was set up and between 1455 and 1456, **Hattorpe-tagune /Behind-Hattorpe Tower** was reconstructed to its 2nd shape (height approx. 20 m, two store and two defence floors).

Intensive buiding works were also carried out on the southern and south-western sides of the town. Between 1453 and 1456, **Karja /Cattle Gate main tower** was built higher and a **2nd foregate complex** set up. Contrary to Harju Gate, the previous foregate complex was demolished here. The new foregate, a modern gatehouse with two side towers and a drawbridge, was built by the former double wall. This complex has been destroyed as well, and the description is based on the aforementioned city map and maquette dating from 1683.

On the south-western side of the city, where the wall mounted uphill, both **Megede** and **Talli towers** were rebuilt between 1455 and 1456. This was unavoidable, since major reconstructions of the fortification system at the Long and Short Leg had begun. From 1450 to 1456, the **Long Leg Gate Tower** was rebuilt more or less into its present shape, between 1454 and 1456, the Short Leg Gate Tower and the section of the **town wall between the gates** were set up in their final locations. To complete the wall between the lower town and Toompea castle, a **60 m section** was built north of the Long Leg Gate between 1454 and 1458. It continued up to the section built around 1311 on Kanne's orders. A small tower called **Seegitagune /Behind-Almshouse Tower** was built there behind the almshouse.

Due to vast differences in the base caused by the strength of the relief, building towers and walls was a complicated technical and military enterprise. The Estonian master builder of the town, Hans Kotke (*Cotke, Kotiken*) with other masters and journeymen succeeded in carrying out the project, funded by alderman Palmedag. First of all, the **Long Leg Gate tower** was reconstructed. When two weather vanes were set on the roof and the hidden portcullis forged in 1456, a typical five-storied gate tower was finished (ground plan 8.2 (8.5) by 8.6 (10.1) m, height approx. 20 m). The new floors could be reached by a winding staircase. In the beginning the tower was named 'the tower before the Long Hill' (... *torne uor deme Langen berge*), but the final name was 'the gate under the Long Dome Hill' (*Pforte unter dem Langen Domberge*), in Estonian Pika Jala väravatorn /Long Leg Gate tower.

The supervisor of the construction of the **Short Leg Gate tower** was alderman Palmedag, after whom the 'new gate at the Short Hill'

Short Leg Gate tower, built in 1454—1456. View from the Short Leg

(*de nie porten vppe deme Korten berge*) was named. Later on, the tower got its final name *'Thor am kleinen Domberge'*, in Estonian Lühikese Jala värav /Short Leg Gate. The lower part of this unique four-storied diamond-shaped tower has been well preserved, while the upper part has been restored. The passageway after which the tower is named winds gradually through the north-eastern side of the ground floor. Originally, there were two portals in the gate, but only one has been preserved. The upper portal was protected also by a portcullis. It is not quite clear how the defenders reached the watch floor. Later on, when

Short Leg Gate tower. View of the gateway

the wall in the vicinity of the work yards was built higher, the southern corner of the tower got a new winding staircase. The exact layout of the upper part of the new town wall by the Long Leg remains unknown. There were certainly loopholes in it, but it is not known how the warriors could move on the sloping (9 per cent) wall. Most probably, there were steps in the defence gallery.

The account book of Tallinn (*Kemmerei-Buch*, 1432—1463) proves that the building of the structurally complex wall mounting by the Long Leg to Toompea was initially funded by alderman Euert Pepersack. He was first mentioned in the records of the city in 1455, but works were started a year earlier. Pepersack gave a bill to the city for the last time in 1456, although the final settlement (*de rekenschopp*) between him and the magistracy was made in January 1457. The accounts were thorough, including a balance statement. The total expenditure had amounted to 5,952 marks.

As mentioned earlier, a small tower was built between the section of the wall near the Long Leg Gate and the earlier built Kanne's wall. The name of the tower, **'the tower behind the almshouse'**, is conventional. Historical documents refer to it simply as 'the tower' or 'the new tower'. The building has been destroyed, but 18th century survey charts prove that this little five-storey tower (∅ 6.8 m, height approx. 16.5 m) represented the type described earlier: a platform on the top, floors united by winding stairs that had become especially fashionable at that time.

Major fortification works were carried out on the **western and north-western sides of the town**, which in the Middle Ages were considered very dangerous in times of war, probably due to the fact that the landscape there provided a favourable location for enemy foothold. For that reason, more towers were built here than to the eastern side. Between 1455 and 1456, **Loewenschede Tower** was reconstructed. **Nun Tower, Sauna Tower** and the section of the **town wall between Golden Foot Tower and the Nun Gate** were also rebuilt around the same time.

The **III Loewenschede Tower** was an interesting example of the type of open towers that had developed in Tallinn. The earlier built walls were strengthened. The new five-storied tower is based on an equilateral triangle (wall up to 2.3 m thick at the ground level, total height 24.2 m). At the time when the tower was built, the town wall section here was low, but a plan to build it higher existed, so there are passages both to the old town wall and the planned new one at the rear of the tower. The passages were lit through a pointed arch shaped niche in the middle of the rear part of the tower. When completed, the tower had one old and two new defence floors, the uppermost one was a platform with a water-tight floor, 11 loopholes and a wide opening for transportation. The builder of the tower, Tideman Louenschede presented a settlement to the magistracy in 1456, which stated 'how much the building of the tower had cost him' (*dat sin toerne gekostet hadde to buwende*).

The **IV Nun Tower** was built partly according to the same scheme, partly following the example of Hellemann and Plate towers. From a saddle tower, it was built into a 3-storied open tower. The plan of the building formed three-quarters of a circle (∅ 9.65 m, height 24.5 m) and a high outer socle. It had a high store floor and two typical defence floors. On the town side there was a pointed arch shaped niche, similar to that of Loewenschede Tower. In the lower part of the niche there was a door leading to the store and a narrow window, in the upper part there was a gallery for the renovated town wall, which also led to the defence floors. In the course of these reconstructions, the section of the

In the Nun Tower — Sauna Tower — Golden Foot Tower section of the town wall consists of parts built in the course of seven centuries. View from the north

town wall between the Golden Foot Tower and the Nun Gate was strengthened, it was buttressed, parapetted and roofed. The thickness of the wall in different sections varied between 2.45 and 2.75 m, average height from the ground was 13 m. As works proceeded, it became necessary to build the Sauna Tower higher. The **IV Sauna Tower** was approx. 18 m high and had a wooden hourding. The original upper part of the tower has not been preserved.

After 1457, fortification works temporarily slowed down. Old debts to the builders were paid, and future plans probably made. In 1461 a decision was taken to strenghthen the weakest links in the town wall, but after that, new type outworks had to be built. This marks the real

beginning of the transition to horizontal fortification. Probably in the early 1460s, the **III Nunnadetagune /Behind-the-Nuns Tower** (re-built upper part, height 19.9 m, timber hourding) and the **III Lippe Tower** (analogous to Nunnadetagune) were built. Soon after that, the relatively weak **wall section between Golden Foot and Rope Hill towers** was strengthened and built higher. From 1461 to 1462, the **Nun Gate** was reconstructed and a **new foregate with one side tower** was built. The gate complex has not survived, but 18th century drawings and later pictures exist which show us what it looked like. The city account book offers plenty of information about the works, which were begun in the spring of 1461, when stones and lime were delivered.

58

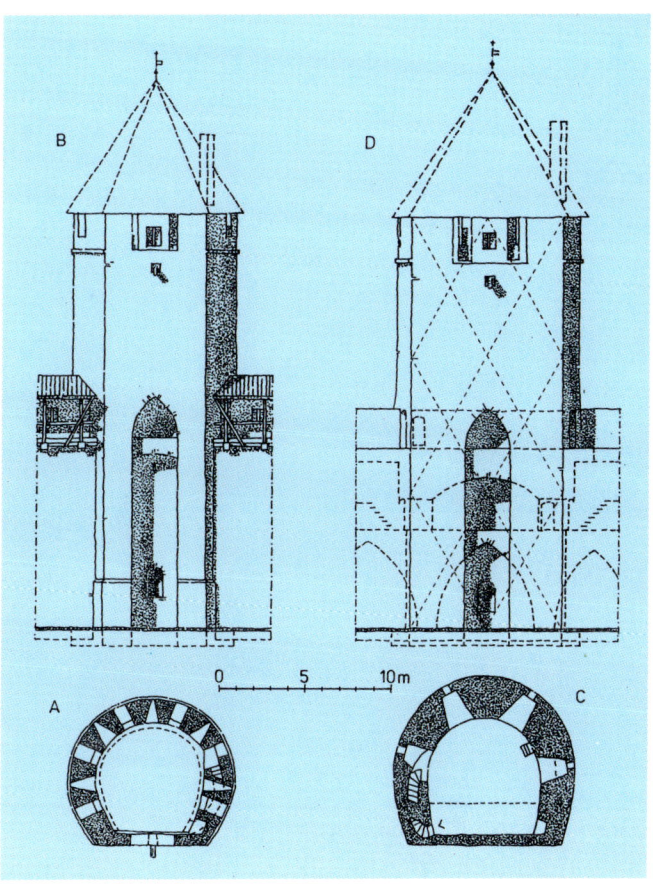

Fortified towers of Tallinn around 1455—56. A — upper defence floor of Nunnatorn /Nun Tower, B — view of the same tower from the town, C — cannon floor of the III Loewenschede Tower, D — view of the same tower from the town
← *Sauna Tower, built in 1371—1372, the upper part renovated in 1898*

Later on, there are several records of the building of the foregate (...*als men de vorporte vor de Susterporten buwede*).

At the same time, walls behind Boleman bathhouse, in the vicinity of the later Kiek in de Kök, were built higher. Many men were employed to carry out these large-scale projects. Barrels of beer and quass, provided to the men by their contracts, were drunk, and much food to go with it eaten. In six weeks, 117 Riga marks were used for food and drink 'before the Nun Gate'. Other entries record the amounts paid for beer, quass, meat, fish, butter, pork fat, salt, etc. The supervisor was city master builder and stone-cutter Hans Kotke. It is known that one

Nun Tower — Sauna Tower — Golden Foot Tower section of the town wall, restored in 1958—1960. View from the south

more Estonian took part in the building, the foreman of the draymen Pauwel Muste (also: *Must, Schwarte*). The result of the work was the 5-storied **main tower of the Nun Gate**, which was a typical open tower with 3 defence floors and a platform. The upper floors could be reached by winding stairs built in the northern side of the tower in the course of fortifying the town wall. In front of the main gate, there were outworks surrounded by high walls, which continued up to the foregate house and its single side tower. Several elements of the gatehouse were similar to those used at Viru foregate. There were two entrances, a big and a small one, they both has drawbridges. According to drawings, the northern side tower was four-storied, with specific holes in the walls for vertical firing. In the course of rebuilding the foregate, an additional **oblique wall** was started by the gate, which followed the slope up to the wall of the Great Castle of Toompea.

At this point, Tallinn was ready to take the next important step in modernising its fortifications. Between 1463 and 1472, a new rampart,

Embrasure in the lower defence floor of the IV Golden Foot Tower, view from the inside

meant for firearms, was built **between the Nun Gate and the Great Coast Gate**. The rampart was 700 m long and had a regular ground plan, its two shorter ends joined the centre at equal angles. First a new moat was dug and surrounded by a palisade from the outside, and by a 2 m high wall firing chambers in it from the inside. This type of wall was called a **firing wall** (*schuttenwall*). On the side of the town, the wall was reinforced with earth dug from the moat that gave the wall extra strength and hid the camouflaged road used by the defenders to transport their cannons and provisions. The wall was named **Nunnavall**

Wooden inner staircase on the lower defence floor of the IV Golden Foot Tower, dating from the 16th or 17th century

/**Nun Wall** (*Systernwall*) later on, and took 10 years to build. Many masters, builders and auxiliary help (*arbetslude*) were employed. During weekends and campaign work, the magistracy supplied free strong and weak beer (*beer, dunnebeer*), as well as food (*vitalie*) to go with it. The completed outworks complex stood on the western and north-western sides of the town for centuries. With a few additions, it has been depicted by Olearius and Merian in their well-known views of the city dating from the end of the 16th and the beginning of the 17th century. These prints were published between 1647 and 1652.

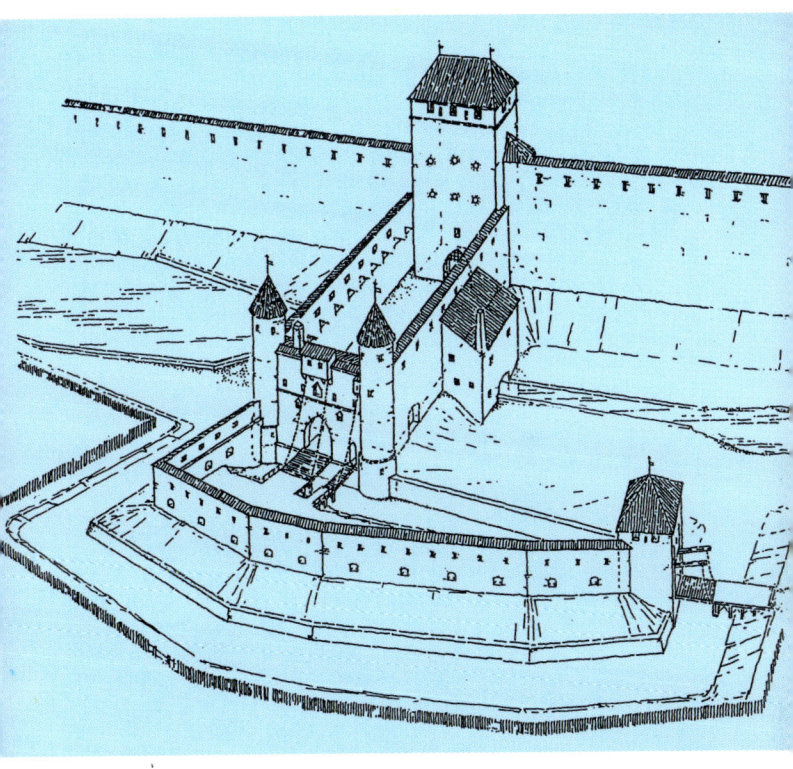

Viru Gate complex after reconstructions in 1471—1473, the Great Zwinger in the foreground (reconstruction)

The earlier built **double wall** (*parcham*) **between the Great and the Small Coast gates** was rebuilt into a similar firing wall. The rear of the wall was filled with earth and buttressed to stand the weight of the earth in 1473. A **palisade between the Small Coast and Viru gates** had been built already in 1468. Between 1471 and 1473, **Viru foregate** was reconstructed. An additional (3rd) bar gate was built. It was a polygonal outwork with a firing wall and a moat, called the **Great Zwinger** (*grote cingele*). In the south, the outworks bordered with the 2nd foregate, built in the middle of the century. The northern side of the Zwinger bordered with a new gatehouse, leading to a bridge over the moat. The yard of the Zwinger, the outworks, were surrounded by a high wall with cannon chambers in it. The lower part of the wall was reinforced with a thick layer of earth. Since old buttressed stone walls already existed between Viru and Harju gates, it is possible to state that by the last quarter of the 15th century, the whole town was surrounded by modernised fortifications, 20—50 m deep outworks.

Cannon chamber on the 3rd floor of the Kiek in de Kök
➜ *Cannon Tower Kiek in de Kök, built in 1475—1483, rebuilt 1693—1697.*
View from the north-west

Followed an important event, the construction of the projecting **I Kiek in de Kök cannon tower** on the south-western side of the city between 1475 and 1476, and the rebuilding of the same tower from 1477 to 1483 (**II Kiek in de Kök**). The tower was erected at a turning point of the old double wall. It was 17.3 m in diameter, its total height, the projecting upper part included, was 37.9 m. Compared to formerly built towers, a number of military technique innovations were introduced in Kiek in de Kök. It had six floors, the lowest one housing an armoury and a magazine. The next four floors were for firing cannons, and the uppermost one was an open platform. The floors were separated by dome vaults and united by a winding staircase. The 3.7—3.9 m thick walls had 24 cannon chambers, equipped in bar log lafettes and 30 holes for small firearms. The wall closest to the town had winding stairs, flues of the numerous chimneys of the tower, and a number of

5 Walls and towers of Tallinn

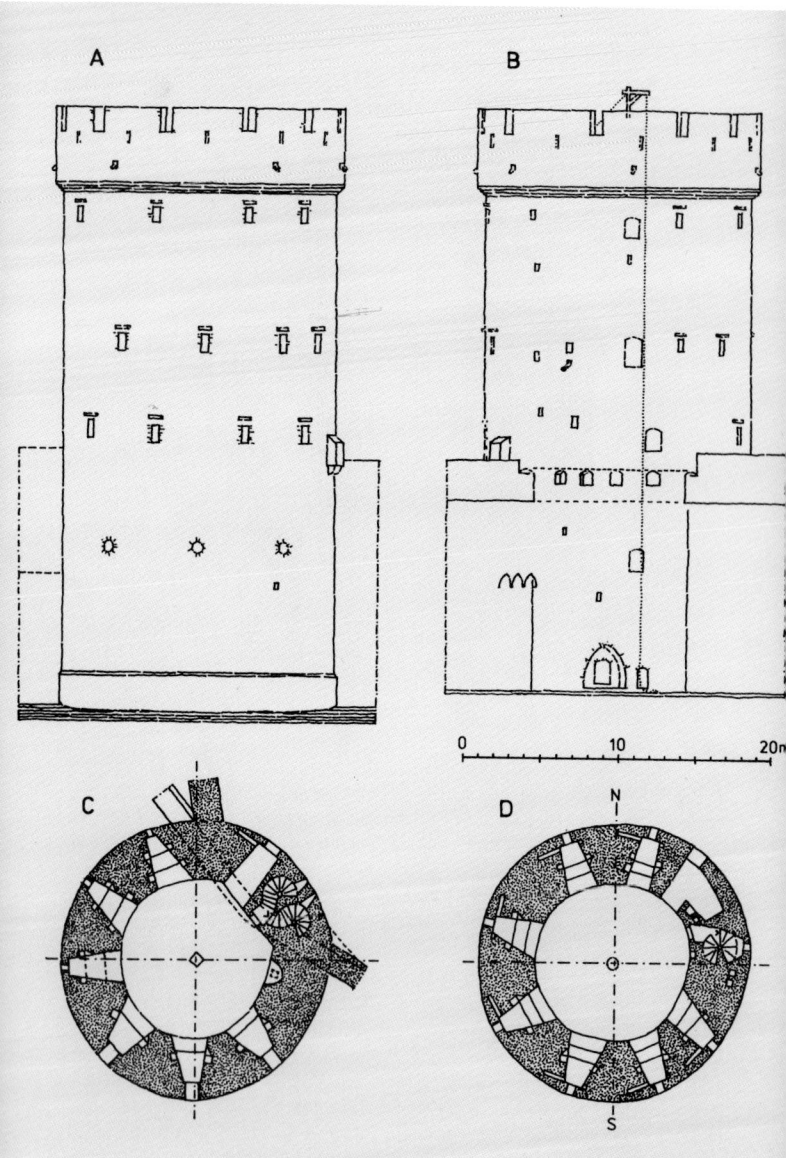

Kiek in de Kök, built in two stages in 1475—1483. A — exterior, B — view from the town, C — ground plan of the 1st floor of the tower (lower defence floor), D — ground plan of the 4th floor of the tower (2nd from top)

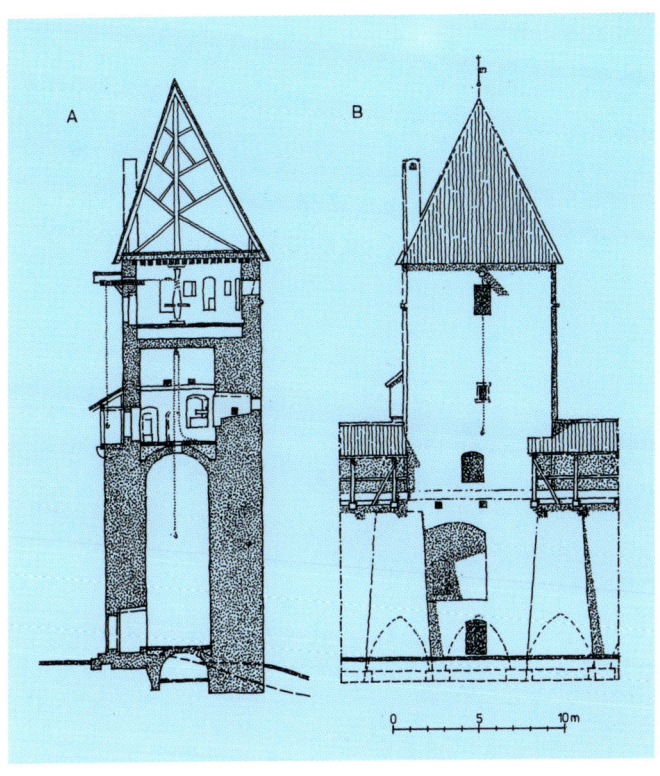

Some towers with rebuilt upper parts from the end of the 15th and the beginning of the 16th century. A — the II Hellemann Tower, completed around 1530, elevation, B — the III Epping Tower, probably completed in 1494—1497, view from the town

auxiliary rooms for the defenders and transport. The transportation openings were in the same wall as well, while another transportation line went through openings on top of the domes. These openings also served as ventilation holes. The rounded floor of the uppermost platform was made watertight by a mixture of sand, tar and birch-oil, which was poured onto the cobbled floor. Rainwater was drained by six water spouts. The name of the tower (*Kiek in de Kök* — peep in the kitchen) dates back to the 16th century and originates from the extraordinary height of the building, it was actually possible to peep into the kitchens of nearby houses through their wide mantle chimneys.

The fire range of the tower covered the outer perimeter, focusing in front of Harju foregate and the area between the fortress and the lower town. It is known that in course of constructing the tower, the surrounding **walls between Karja /Cattle Gate and the Short Leg**

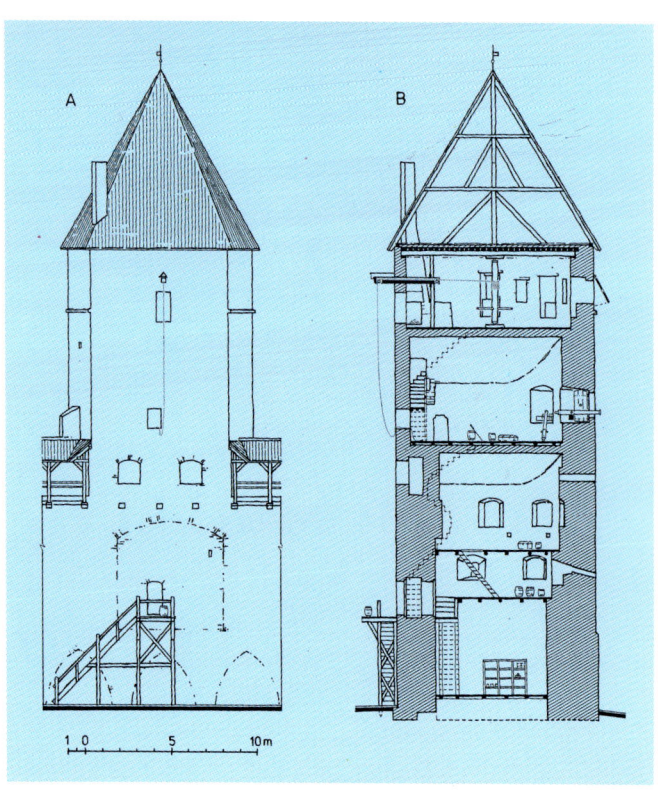

III Köismäe /Rope Hill Tower, probably completed in 1494—1497. A — view from town, B — elevation. Magazine and arsenal on three lower floors, two upper floors used for defence purposes

Gate were built higher (3rd stage of the wall?). **Assauwe** and **Talli towers** were built higher as well (3rd stages?). These works reflect the fear of a conflict between the Livonian Order and Pskov Duchy, which actually resulted in a war in southern Estonia between 1480 and 1481.

Between 1481 and 1490, many towers and sections of the wall were reconstructed. The most extensive works were carried out **in the vicinity of Kuraditorn /Devil Tower**. It was very difficult to build the founding near the moat. The new wall was therefore founded on poles and floats, and it was buttressed from the outside. As far as we know, this was the highest ever built section of the town wall in Tallinn (walls 3 m thick at the ground, total height 15.9 m). The final stage of the **tower by the old Russian church** (*thorn by der russchen kerken*), consisting of 4 floors, was completed in 1487. The upper defence floor had a cantilevered machicolation. The same technique was used in rebuilding the upper part of the **Tall Hermann** in the Small Castle of Toompea, which was carried out around the same time when Kiek in de Kök was built in the lower town. The tower by the old Russian church got a tiled roof, and master painter Diderich van Katwich had been paid for the gilding of the weather vane (... *vor den staningen to vo(r)gulden*) in 1487 year. The year 1491 marked the beginning of the reconstruction of the **town wall between the Nun Gate and the Long Leg Gate**, in 1491—1493, **Saunatagune torn (the tower behind the sauna)** was built there (∅ 9.6—9.8 m, height approx. 19 m, five floors). The name of the tower was first recorded in a list compiled in 1507—1512 (*de nye torne achter demm stauen...*), it might have been called simply the new tower to begin with.

The following very short quiet period ended soon. Between 1494 and 1497, several other fortification works had to be carried out for fear of a Russian siege. The main aim of the works seems to have been preparing the outworks of the town for attack. Several sections of the town wall were probably built higher. In course of these works, three towers in the encircling wall were reconstructed a couple of years later: the **IV Golden Foot Tower** (height 22.5 m, five floors), the **III Epping Tower** (height 22.5 m, five floors) and the **III Rope Hill Tower** (height 26.5 m, three magazine and two defence floors). The lower floors of the towers were built in the 15th century style, but the upper floors had timber flooring, log ceilings and permanent roofs. No more open platforms were built. The wide transport openings were replaced by narrow arch-lintelled holes, through which the logs with pulley blocks projected. The upper floors were thus adjusted for firearms, catapults were no longer used there.

For the same reasons, the **main tower of Viru Gate** was reconstructed extensively at the turn of the 15th and 16th centuries. The tower probably got its final shape then (ground plan 11.3 by 9.3 m, height 22 m, five floors). The **main tower of the Great Coast Gate** was rebuilt as well (height 20.5 m, six floors).

But peace time did not last. Between 1510 and 1512, as well as a few years later, works were carried out at the **Great Coast Gate**. The building was speeded up in 1518 because an attack 'by the Danish king and his people' was feared. During the following 11 years, the **foregate complex of the Great Coast Gate** was completely rebuilt. A new foregate house was built, and the upper part of the western tower reconstructed. A mighty cannon tower, then named simply Zwinger, was built at the site of the former eastern tower. It was later known as **Rosenkrantz**, finally **Paks Margareeta /Fat Margaret**. A new rampart was built between the cannon tower and Stolting Tower, this became the **eastern wall of the outworks**. Most masonry works were carried out between 1518 and 1526, carpenter works in the following 3 years. The complex was probably designed by a Polish master builder, Clemens Pale. From 1522, supervision was taken over by Gert Konigk, a master builder from Münster, who cut a fine Gothic tardif style dolomite coat of arms of the landlord, the Livonian Order, and placed it on the gatehouse in 1529. The complex was thus completed. It included a

The fortified Great Coast Gate complex after the 3rd foregate and the zwinger (cannon tower and rampart) had been completed in 1518—1529 (reconstruction)

cannon tower based on three-quarters of a circle (25 m outside, 12.5 m inside). The tower was located on the steep edge of the coast, and was therefore 16 m high in the west and 22 m in the east. It had three floors for cannons, and an open platform above them. The platform was surrounded by a double gallery in the rounded part. The outer wall of the gallery was based on a pointed arch-shaped machicolated moulding, which had loopholes in it. Inserted ceilings of the main floors were wooden, they were based on projections in the walls and a limestone post in the middle.

There were 22 firing chambers (embrasures) in the tower, all equipped with flues to ventilate gunpowder smoke. The new gatehouse had three floors, the Tudor-arched portal could be closed by means of a protcullis and a double door. The door could be barred from the inside. In protecting the pier and the roadstead, the eastern wall of the Zwing-

Dolomite coat-of-arms on the 3rd foregate building of the Great Coast Gate.
Originally the coat-of-arms was painted
➔ *The 3rd foregate of the Great Coast Gate with the Rosenkrantz (Fat Margaret)*
cannon tower, the upper part rebuilt in the end of 17th century

er, the so-called firing wall (*schuttenwall*, 3 m thick at the ground, height 10 m), played an important part. There were 10 cannon chambers in the lower belt of the wall, the upper roofed parapet had traditional loopholes in it. Altogether, there were 32 holes for cannons and about 124 for small firearms in the new fortification complex. The cannon fire was mainly aimed eastwards, towards the bay, roadstead and piers. The Port Tower offered some defence, but in case of a military conflict, it was rather weak.

The construction of the described Zwinger marked the final stage of transition to horizontal defence. Since the Reformation, marking the beginning of modern times, reached Tallinn exactly by the time the Zwinger was built, we can conclude the following about **medieval fortifications of Tallinn**.

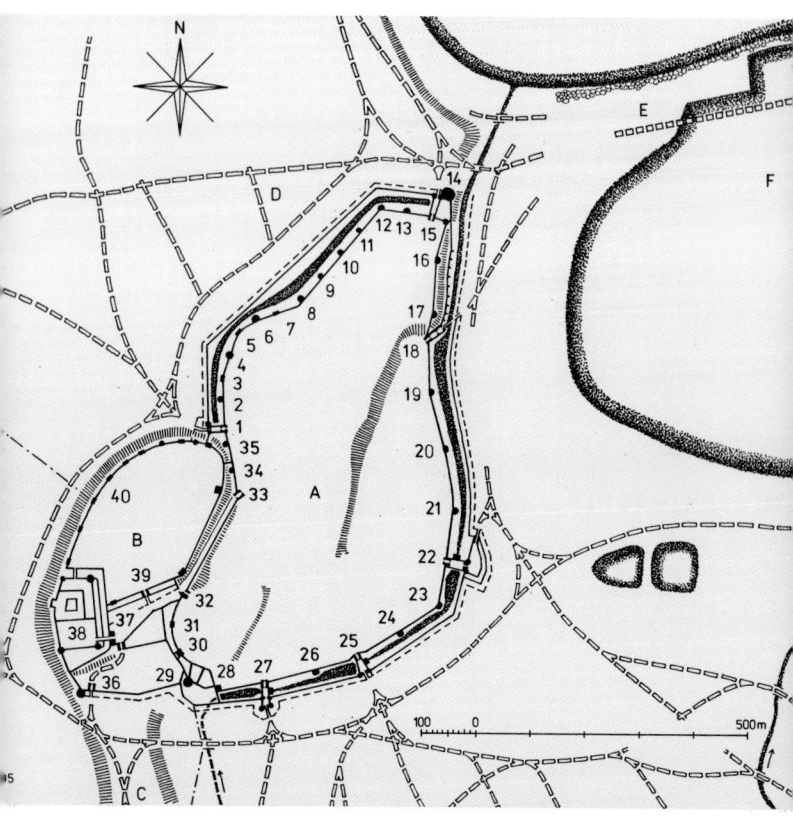

Topographical scheme of Tallinn at the end of the Middle Ages, approx. 1530 (reconstruction). A — lower town, B — Toompea, C — Tõnismägi, D — Köismäe /Rope Hill suburb (Reperbahn), E — port, F — Tallinn Bay, G — the Härjapea River, 1 —Nunnavärav /Nun Gate, 2 — Nunnatorn /Nun Tower, 3 — Sauna Tower, 4 —Kuldjala /Golden Foot Tower, 5 — Nunnadetagune /Behind-the-Nuns Tower, 6 — Loewenschede Tower, 7 — Lippe Tower, 8 — Köismäe /Rope Hill Tower, 9 — Plate Tower, 10 — Epping Tower, 11 — Grusbeke-tagune /Behind-Grusbeke Tower, 12 — Renten Tower, 13 — Wulfardi-tagune /Behind-Wulfard Tower, 14 — the fortified complex of the Great Coast Gate, 15 — Stolting Tower, 16 — Hattorpe-tagune /Behind-Hattorpe Tower, 17 — the tower by the old Russian church, 18 — the Small Coast Gate, 19 — Bremen Tower, 20 — Munkadetagune /Behind-the-Monks, 21 — Hellemann Tower, 22 — Viru Gate fortified complex, 23 — Hinke Tower, 24 — Kuraditorn /Devil Tower, 25 — Karja /Cattle Gate, 26 — Assauwe Tower, 27 — Harju Gate, 28 — Kitsetorn /Goat Tower, 29 — Kiek in de Kök, 30 — Megede Tower, 31 —Talli Tower, 32 — Short Leg Gate, 33 — Long Leg Gate, 34 — Seegitagune /the tower behind the almshouse, 35 — Saunatagune /the tower behind the sauna, 36 — Foregate of the Order Castle and the Rosenkrantz, 37 — moat , walls and gates in the outer ward of the castle, 38 — the Order Castle, 39 — Toomvärav /Toom Gate, 40 — wall and towers of the Episcopal Castle. Steeper

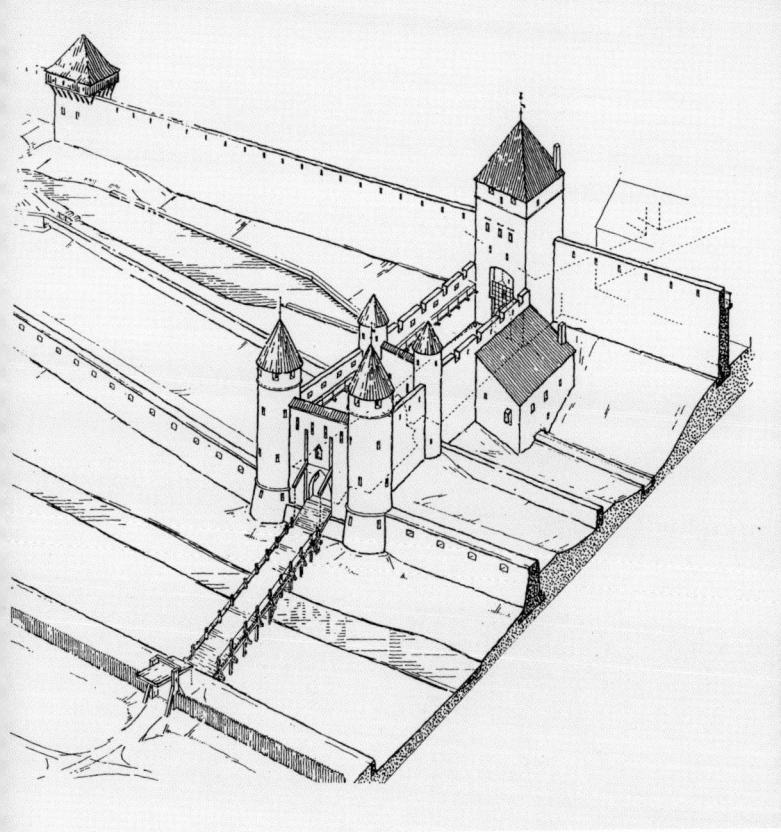

*slopes, border between the lower town and the Order Castle, streets around the
centre of the town and the coast line of that time are shown.
Harju Gate fortification complex in approx. 1540, before the gate was closed
(reconstruction)*

The area of the lower town in the 1530s was 29.3 hectares. The
whole area was surrounded by 11 hectares of outworks, which were
parted and independent from the fortress of Toompea, although located
by the hill. The encircling wall was 2.35 km long, or 2.7 km when
including the double walls and the foregate walls. There were 8 gate
towers, 11 foregate towers and 27 defence towers in the wall, altogether 64. They were between 18 and 24 m high on the average, but Rope
Hill Tower was 26.5 m, Kiek in de Kök 37.9 m high. The encircling
wall was 2.15—3.0 m thick and up to 15.9 m high. Most of the perimeter was surrounded by a 2.25 km long main moat, which was filled
with water and dammed in some parts. There were three water mills on
the moat and 7 bridges across it. The main moat was surrounded by

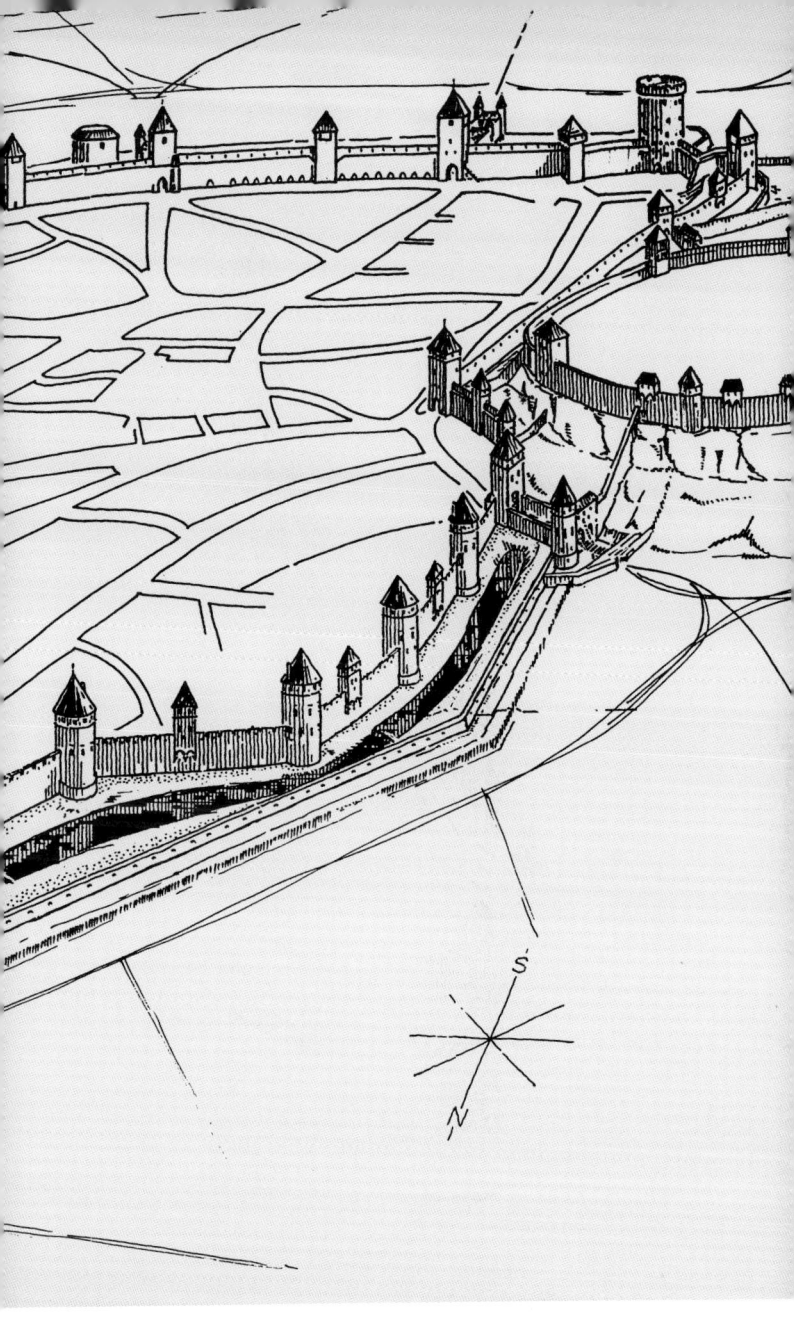

Fortified zone of the lower town of Tallinn in 1538. View from the north-west (reconstruction)

earthworks, which in some parts bordered with another moat.

The fortifications of the lower town were strengthened by the hilltop fortress of Toompea, which belonged to the Livonian Order. At the end of the Middle Ages, the 7.4 hectare area of the castle was encircled by a 1.1 km wall. Including the inner walls, the total length of the walls of Toompea was 2.0 km. On the southern side of the castle there were 2.2 hectares of outworks, including 0.5 km of earthworks, the foregate of the castle was protected by a cannon tower named Rosenkrantz (not to be confused with the tower Fat Margaret, which in the Swedish era had a similar name). Altogether, the castle seems to have had 23 defence towers and gates. The centre of Tallinn was thus encircled by a strong and wide (14.2 ha) defence zone at the end of the Middle Ages. Including the Port Tower, it had approximately 70 towers and gates.

The described fortifications are a major accomplishment of medieval architecture in Estonia. The fortifications of Tallinn are an excellent example of the Nordic simple and discrete architectural style with little but tasteful décor. Fortification architecture was directly influenced by its technical and functional side, which depended on the typological development of fortification. The development of the local architecture depended mostly on the building material and the traditions and skills of handling it. The main building material was hard, slabby limestone from northern Estonia. Excellent use was made of the characteristics of its different layers. Since all of the nearly 40 layers of limestone that had been cut had been tried out throughout history, master builders knew exactly which layer could be used for floor slabs, which for brackets or cantilevers, which for steps, which for regular building stone, and which layers could be used only for lime burning. Timber constructions had an important part in the architecture as well. Different kinds of timber were skilfully combined with stone. All these skills were passed on from generation to generation by master builders, who had gathered in trade 'boards' (*Amt*). By the end of the 14th century, we can already talk about **an independent Tallinn school of architecture**. Since the same masters supervised profane, sacral and military buildings, the Gothic stone architecture of Tallinn was understandably universal in nature. Same or similar techniques and constructions were used in different types of buildings.

Fortification works continued. Soon after the Reformation, in 1532, the erection of half-circular or polygonal earthworks, the so-called **High Roundel** (*Hoge Roundel*) was started around Kiek in de Kök. The roundel was built by master builder Henning, who was specially invited from Hildesheim, Germany. Inside the roundel there was a stone wall with cannon chambers. From the outside, the roundel was reinforced with earth. In the course of building, the defence was doubled here and 15—18 m of the foot of Kiek in de Kök was protected by a high earth wall. In 1533, the roundel was united with the **new rampart**, which continued up until **Harju Gate**, and was prolonged towards **Cattle Gate** in 1538. A new foregate called the **rampart gate** was cut through the earthworks. A new **cannon tower, Lurenburg** ($\varnothing$ 20.4 m, height approx. 18 m, three storeys), was built in line with the moat to protect the gate. This horse-shoe shaped tower reminded of the earlier described Zwinger at the Great Coast Gate (Fat Margaret).

In 1558, the Livonian War began, which lasted until 1583. Several battles were fought in the vicinity of Tallinn. According to Balthasar Russow, a chronicler of the time, the town was fortified carefully. At the beginning of the war, the **Zwinger at the Viru Gate** was reconstructed into a **roundel**. The earlier polygonal ground plan was preserved, and the roundel kept the formerly built foregate in its northern corner. The new rampart between the roundel and Cattle Gate was completed, and **Harju Gate** was closed, since it didn't meet the new defence requirements. **Two new-Italian type bastions** were built on the southern side of Toompea during the war.

While preparing for the war, the **rampart between Viru and the Small Coast gate** was reconstructed as well. **Two old-Italian type bastions** were built at the turning point of the rampart **between the Great Coast Gate and the Nun Gate** (the Nun Wall). Later on, the bastions were named **Sõnnikukast /Manure Case** (*Mesekast*) and **Lõvilinnus /Lion Burg** (*Louwenborch*). A small **triangle-based fort** (*schanz*) was built on the eastern side of the Great Coast Gate Zwinger. At the same time, a former seaside park, the so-called **Rose Garden** (*Rosengarden*) was transferred into a cannon fort. A **major part of the town wall and its towers** were modernised as well. The open defence platforms of the medieval towers were liquidated. They were built somewhat higher, and got permanent ceilings and roofs. Loopholes were lintelled, big transportation openings narrowed. The lower parts of several towers were taken into use as magazines or arsenals. Since the active war front had been transferred to the ramparts and the range of cannon fire had increased a great deal, several towers were transferred into cannon fire spots in the depth of the defence system (**Devil Tower, Hellemann Tower, Hinke Tower**, later **Golden Foot Tower**). The town wall was built higher in several sections where it was considered unavoidable. The upper part of **Kiek in de Kök** was rebuilt, it got a new defence gallery.

1561—1710: THE SWEDISH ERA

The first battle within the walls of Tallinn was fought in June 1561, when the city voluntarily surrendered to Sweden. First the castle was taken by intensive cannon fire from the lower town. One of the corner towers of the order Castle, **Stür den Kerl** was hit and destroyed, as well as the upper part of another tower, **Landskrone**.

A little later, the eastern side of the town and the **Great Coast Gate** were "baptised by fire". In June 1569, a joined fleet of Denmark and Lubeck arrived at the roadstead of Tallinn. They plundered and pirateered nearly 150 ships belonging to the citizens and the port of Tallinn. During 13 days, the city was under constant fire. With favourable winds, the ships then disappeared as suddenly as they had appeared. According to Russow, the port of Tallinn looked like ' ... a sad mother whose children have been kidnapped' after the attack.

79

Between 1570 and 1571, Tallinn was sieged by Magnus, brother of the King of Denmark, who had joined forces with the Russian Czar Ivan IV. The city was sieged for 7 months, during which several attempts were made to cut the town from the port. As the town was very well fortified at the time, the siege was not successful. Another siege was attempted in January and February of 1577 by Russian forces. This time, the southern side of the town was under most intensive fire. The upper part of **Kiek in de Kök** was partly destroyed, all southern and south-western towers suffered some damage, including the **Tall Hermann**, the temporarily repaired **Stür den Kerl, Talli, Megede towers, Short Leg Gate tower** and **Goat Tower**. After the war, most of the damages were taken care of, and several sections of the town wall repaired. For example, the lower part of **Golden Foot Tower** was rebuilt into a magazine in 1598. Most gate complexes were reviewed and rebuilt. The **Great Coast Gate** got a **4th foregate** between 1603 and 1609. The new gate was 10 metres from the third. A similar **foregate** was built at the **Nun Gate** in 1609. Both forgates were built by the town master builder Arendt Passer. Neither of them is depicted in Olearius' or Merian's views of the north-western part of the city, which were published between 1647 and 1652. Most probably, their engravings were based on some older drawings by anonymous authors, dating from 1590—1600.

A severe depression in the economic life of Tallinn followed, a relief came only in the mid-17th century. Between 1640 and 1650, the

Tallinn in 1590—1600. Copy of a print by M. Merian from 1652

first sconce in Tallinn was erected. This was the **Horn Bastion** in front of the Fat Margaret. At the same time, **the weakest rampart** on the eastern side of the town was reconstructed. After a few years, **two Dutch type bastions (Himsel bastions)** were set up. The area between the earthworks and the town wall was levelled and divided into building lots. The first street outside the old centre was formed (Uus /New Street). The construction of a bastional front intensified especially in the 1680s, due to the political instability, which in 1700 led to the Great Northern War. Because of the economic recession and the beginning of the war, fortifications were built on a smaller scale than planned.

The rebuilding of the town wall was an important part of the modernisation of fortifications. Three former cannon towers, **Kiek in de Kök, Lurenburg** and **Rosenkrantz (Fat Margaret)** were transformed into powerful cannon fire points amidst the defence zone. Kiek in de Kök was made easier to access via new entrances and staircases, new firing cambers for wheeled cannons were built, and the 6th floor reconstructed. A mighty cone-shaped dome was built on the new walls of the sixth floor, which now were 3.7 m thick. The new ceiling and roof were 2—3.5 m thick, and the height of the tower 45 m. **Rosenkrantz Tower** (*Rosen Krantz*) at the Great Coast Gate was reconstructed, the machicolation and the defence galleries were demolished and replaced by a new cannon floor. The ceiling of the latter was made of logs and stone slabs. **Lurenburg Tower** was probably rebuilt in a similar fashion.

Unfortunately, all the work carried out by Sweden and its provin-

81

Nun Gate complex (main gate tower with two foregates) in 1865. Oil by E. H. Schlichting. Estonian Art Museum

cial city of Tallinn (*Reval*) turned out to be useless. When the city, which was disturbed by plague, surrendered to Russia in 1710, most of the population of the town had died. 500 men of the 4,000-man garrison had survived.

1710—1918: THE RUSSIAN ERA

After the war and the recovery of the economy of the city, the fortifications of Tallinn were stocked. Plans of the State Military Units Tallinn Engineering Detachment, dating from 1728 and 1738, prove that Renten Tower, Behind-Wulfard Tower and Goat Tower were in ruins. Since priority was given to ramparts when building new fortifications, the old towers were kept mostly for their utilitarian value. At the same time, demolishing of towers began. The first to be demolished was **Lurenburg cannon tower** (1767). The **Small Coast Gate** (1779) and the **Great Coast main gate** (1728) followed shortly. At the beginning of the next century, **Lippe Tower, Viru main gate tower** (1843), **Cattle Gate** (1849) and the **tower behind the Russian church** (around 1854) were demolished. After the Crimean War (1854—1855), Tallinn was removed from the list of land forts and most of the buildings were handed over to the city. The historical defence function of the

Opening in the town wall on Suur-Kloostri Street. The gateway reminding of a Gothic triumph arch was designed by architect W. Neumann in 1896—1897

medieval walls and towers of Tallinn was over.

After that, many defence buildings were demolished quickly. Technical, practical and aesthetic reasons explained the demolishing. **Most of Harju Gate** was demolished in 1862, the original **Nun Gate complex** in 1868, most of **Behind-Wulfard** in 1870, and the last **(4th) foregate of the Great Coast Gate** in the same year. In 1875, the remainders of **Harju main gate** were pulled down, in 1880 what was left of **Renten Tower**. In 1882 **Devil Tower** was demolished, in 1887 the remnants of the **Small Coast Gate**. In 1888, **Viru (2nd) foregate** was pulled down to build the horse tramway. **Seegitagune torn /Behind-the-Almshouse Tower** and **Saunatagune /Behind-the-Sauna Tower** were demolished as well. Only 26 towers and 1.85 km of town wall were preserved. Medieval moats and earthworks were either completely levelled or had been destroyed. The losses were extensive, what wars and centuries could not accomplish, citizens took care of in a couple of decades.

In mid-19th century, several Baltic German historians and architects (P. E. Jordan, F. G. von Bunge, E. von Nottbeck, W. Neumann and others) protested against the destruction of the historical buildings of Tallinn. They also wrote the first research papers on the history of Tallinn and its heritage. These works resulted in an increasing interest in the

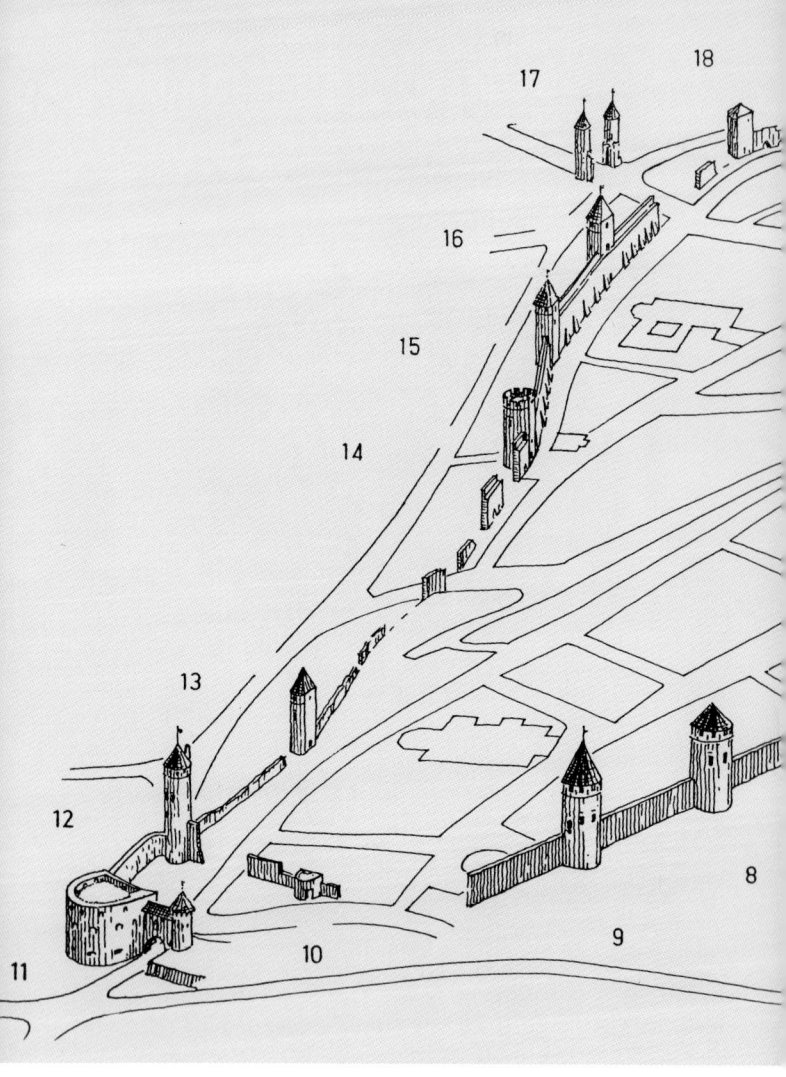

Medieval fortifications of the lower town of Tallinn that have been preserved to present day. 1 — Nunnatorn /Nun Tower, 2 — Sauna Tower, 3 — Kuldjala /Golden Foot Tower, 4 — Nunnadetagune /Behind-the-Nuns Tower, 5 — Loewenschede Tower, 6 — Köismäe /Rope Hill Tower, 7 — Plate Tower, 8 — Epping Tower, 9 — Grusbeke-tagune /Behind-Grusbeke, 10 — remains of Wulfarditagune /Behind-Wulfard Tower, 11 — the Great Coast foregate and Fat Margaret zwinger,

12 — Stolting Tower, 13 —Hattorpe-tagune /Behind-Hattorpe Tower, 14 — Bremen Tower, 15 — Munkadetagune /Behind-the-Monks Tower, 16 — Hellemann Tower, 17 — side towers of Viru foregate, 18 — Hinke Tower, 19 — Assauwe Tower, 20 — remains of Kitsetorn /Goat Tower, 21 — Kiek in de Kök, 22 — Megede Tower, 23 — Talli Tower, 24 — Short Leg Gate tower, 25 — Long Leg Gate tower, 26 — remains of the tower behind the sauna

Kiek in de Kök museum. Inside view

heritage. At the end of the 19th century, the first restoration works were carried out. To improve the traffic between the old town and the railway station, the **town wall** was opened by Suur-Kloostri Street in 1896—1897. The gateway that reminded of a Gothic-style triumph arch was designed by W. Neumann. The parapet of the town wall in this section was reconstructed as well. A. Howen added to the composition in 1898, by restoring the upper part of the **Sauna Tower**, following the example of the Behind-the-Nuns.

1918—1940: THE REPUBLIC OF ESTONIA

After the Republic of Estonia had been proclaimed, Tallinn became its capital. The Heritage Act took effect in 1925. Soon after that, the heritage authorities started to work on the old towers and walls, which had long belonged to no one and had started to decay. One of the major works was the conservation of the upper part of the **town wall near Laboratooriumi Street** in the 1930s. The **towers by Tornide Väljak/ the Square of Towers** got new tiled roofs, the upper part of

Kiek in de Kök and Megede Tower. View from the Freedom Square
→ *Megede Tower (Virgin Tower), restored and built into a café. View from the Danish King's garden, in the background Kiek in de Kök*

Upper part of the restored Talli Tower

Behind-Grusbeke was rebuilt. The reconstruction of several towers into museums was discussed, this included turning **Kiek in de Kök** into a museum of the War of Independence. Due to the outbreak of World War II, these plans were put into practice only at the **Great Coast Gate**, where a part of the complex destroyed by fire in 1917 was restored into the City Museum between 1938 and 1940.

1940—1991: THE SOVIET OCCUPATION

As a result of a political deal between Germany and the USSR from 1939, Estonia was occupied by the Soviet Union in 1940 and forced to apply for membership in the union. Tallinn centre was severely damaged in World War II, approximately one half of the buildings were destroyed. The old town suffered damages in many parts. In 1947, architectural monuments were put under protection. This included the town wall and its towers. In 1959, a special research and building insti-

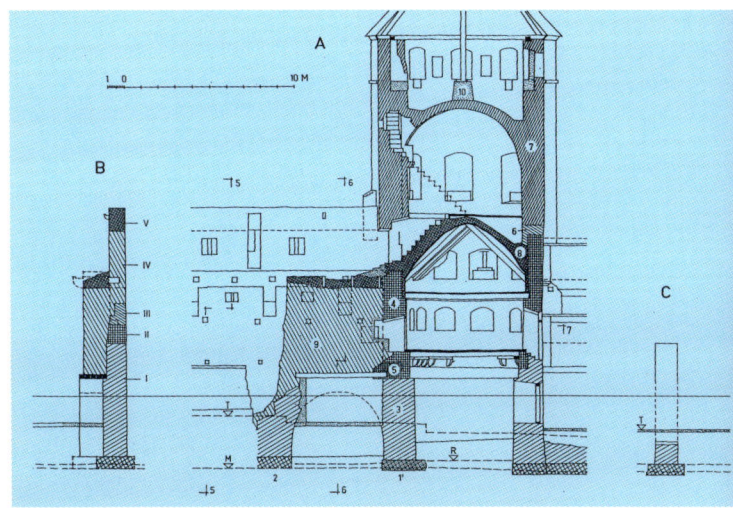

Example of archaeological research into the fortifications of Tallinn (R.Zobel, 1980, p.43). A — elevation of Kuldjala /Golden Foot Tower and the southern section of the town wall, B — cross section of the southern town wall, C — cross section of the older northern part of the wall, T — present profile of ground, R — profile of ground in the Middle Ages, M — original (untouched) ground, 1... 10 — relative chronology of the different building stages of the tower and the walls, I...V — different construction stages of the southern section of the town wall between Sauna and Golden Foot towers

tution, the Restoration Workshop was established to restore and take care of the heritage. Later on, this institution was reorganised into the State Institute for Heritage Planning and the Restoration Board with its branches. In 1951, the restoration of the town wall began, and in 1954, the first historical research backing up the works was started. From then on, several major projects were carried out. The following buildings were conserved and partly restored: the upper part of the **Nun Tower** (1954—1955), the upper part of **Assauwe Tower** (1955), the **town wall section between Talli and Megede towers** (1959 and 1960), **Bremen Tower** (1957), **a section of the town wall by Vene Street** (1959), **Kiek in de Kök** (1957—1959), **the town wall between the Nun Gate and the Golden Foot** (1958—1960), the upper parts and roofs of **Golden Foot, Behind-the-Nuns, Plate, Behind-Grusbeke, Rope Hill** and **Stolting towers** (1962—1967), the **decaying Hellemann Tower** and the **town wall section from the tower to Viru Street** (1962—1967, 1984—1985). **Kiek in de Kök** was made into a museum (1966—1968), **Megede Tower** was built into a café and the neighbouring **walls and Talli Tower** restored (1968—1980), the **Great Coast Gate complex** and the **Fat Margaret** were rebuilt to house the Maritime Museum (1978—1980). Between 1969 and 1983, the decay-

91

Restored Talli Tower, Megede Tower and Kiek in de Kök. View from the north-west

ing of **Loewenschede Tower** was stopped, its upper part was restored and lower part reconstructed. Somewhat later, the **Behind-the-Monks** was restored into a club and a gallery (1979—1982, 1993). The **Short Leg Gate tower** came to be used as a music room and a concert place (1985—1988). Other minor works were carried out as well.

The restoration works were, as a rule, accompanied by thorough research into both historically documented and field data. Archeological, geological and topographical data was researched as well. A trustworthy data base was thus created, and this permits scientific research into the fortifications of medieval Tallinn.

SINCE 1991: THE REPUBLIC OF ESTONIA

The Singing Revolution, the Estonian bloodless fight for independence, which began in 1988, freed Estonia from the Soviet occupation. It united the politically dispersed 'country people' (as Estonians had been calling themselves since the 13th century), many of whom were scattered around the world, and led to the hoisting of the blue, black and white national flag on the Tall Hermann on February 24, 1989, and to the restoration of the Republic of Estonia *de jure et de facto* on August 30, 1991. All state institutions, including those for the preservation of heritage, were reorganised. The State Heritage Department was established in 1993, the new Heritage Act was adopted and took effect in 1994.

Short Leg Gate tower. Renovation of the tiling

The former State Institute for Heritage Planning was divided into several smaller units. Privatising and property restitution processes have intensified building activities everywhere, including the old town. Between 1992 and 1993, repair works at the town wall were started. Many roofs that had been destroyed by storms and cold were restored, over 30 years had passed since the pervious time this work was undertaken. Historical documents prove that in the Middle Ages also roofs did not last longer than that. The town wall of Tallinn and its towers will need constant attention also in the future.

SUMMARY

This book has dealt with the detailed development of medieval Tallinn and its fortifications during a thousand years. For nearly 800 years, from its founding to its demilitarisation, Tallinn was a real burg, its planning and architecture highly dependent on the surrounding fortification zone. The latter, in its turn, depended on the arms and military techniques used. Throughout history, these changed, together with the rulers. In Tallinn, this process was very complicated, full of colourful events and wars, poverty and wealth, ups and downs. In all those years, the town was continuously fortified, repaired and rebuilt. The finely proportioned and technically skilfully completed limestone towers of Tallinn, and kilometres of town wall are, first and foremost, a monument to their builders.

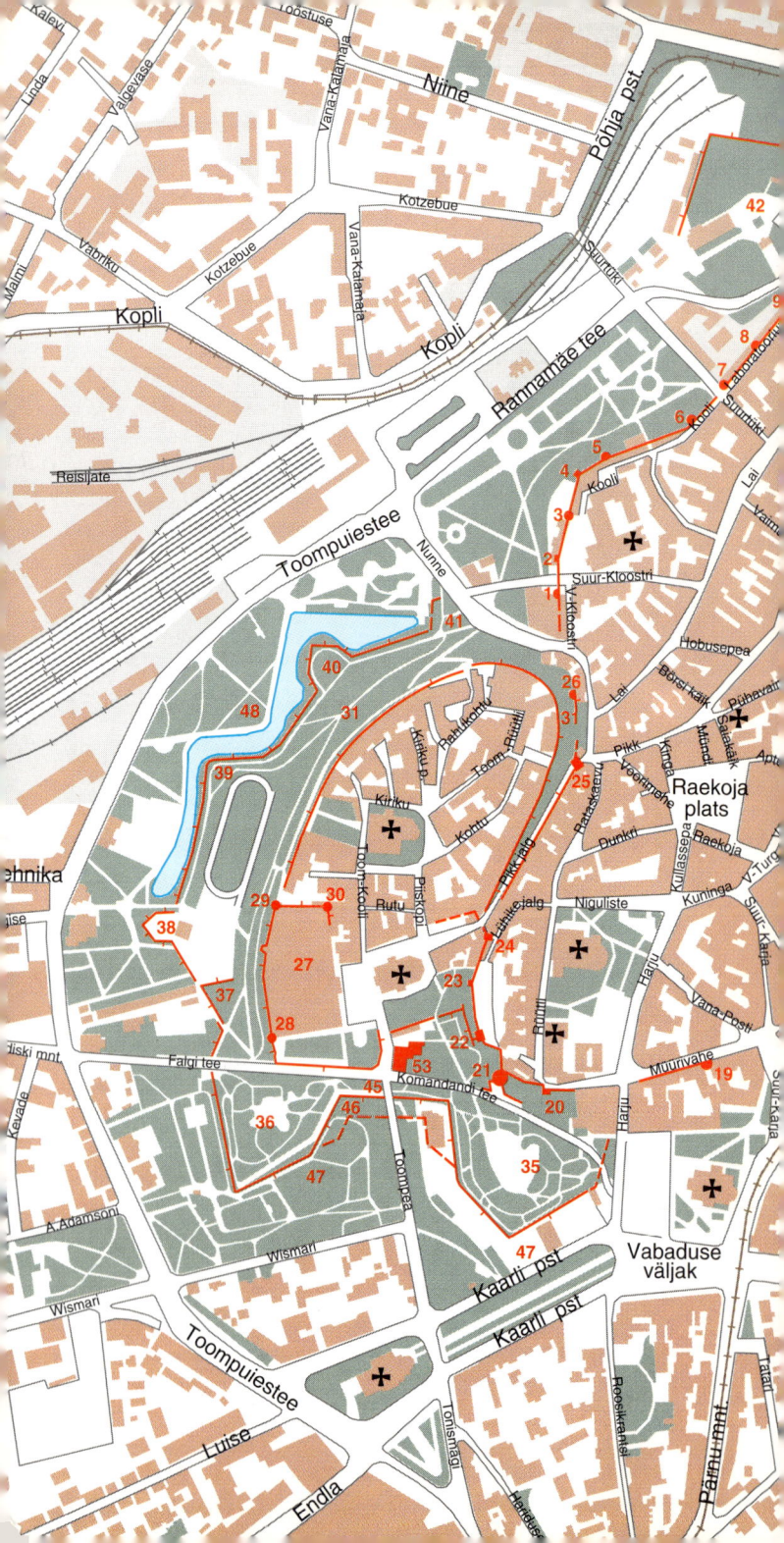